LAVERDA

LAVERDA

RAYMOND AINSCOE

WITH TIM PARKER

OSPREY
AUTOMOTIVE

Published in 1991 by Osprey Publishing,
59 Grosvenor Street, London W1X 9DA

British Library Cataloguing in Publication Data:

A catalogue record for this book is available from the British
Library.

ISBN 1-85532-183-1

Editor Shaun Barrington
Page design Gwyn Lewis
Phototypeset by Keyspools Ltd.
Printed by BAS Printers Limited, Over Wallop, Hampshire

FRONT COVER Laverda SFC; the purpose-built racer that
first appeared in 1971. Just 549 were built.
(Don Morley)

BACK COVER 1982 120 Jota, considered by many to be the
finest three-cylinder Laverda ever made; a very rare
machine. (Tim Parker)

HALF TITLE 75cc Laverda Sport in race trim and colours.
(*In Moto*).

TITLE PAGE The racing machine that was never really
tested, the endurance vee-six; an intriguing part of the
Laverda story. With the right investment, would it
have been a world-beater?

Contents

About the Authors

Raymond Ainscoe has been enthralled by motorcycles since his first visit to the Isle of Man TT races in 1959 as a five-year-old. He is a particular enthusiast of classic Italian racing motorcycles and contributes articles covering a wide range of Italian bikes to *Classic Racer* magazine. This is his second book; his first was *Gilera Road Racers* (Osprey).

Raymond and his wife live in Ilkley with a dwindling bank balance financing a remarkable collection of Italian motorcycles, including a 98cc Laverda, a Rumi Junior and a Gilera Sanremo. He participated in the 1990 edition of the Giro d'Italia as the only foreign entrant aboard a Guzzi Airone.

Tim Parker was born 26.6.47 in Cambridge; a car enthusiast since a baby (particularly motor racing) he added motorcycle enthusiasm in the early 1970s. He bought a Laverda 750 SF2 in 1974 and has owned many motorcycles since. Today he has ten Laverdas; the earliest a 1957 100 Turismo; the latest are a couple of 1984 models, an RGS and LB 125 Sport, with a pair of 750 SFCs for good measure. He's also an avid collector of Laverda memorabilia.

He wrote and published himself The Green Book – *Laverda Twin and Triple Repair and Tune-up Guide* – and wrote, for the Laverda factory, the 1000 RGS official manual which was translated into Italian. Two Osprey titles have reproduced his photographs, *Italian Motorcycles* and *Japanese Motorcycles*.

Tim road races a 750 SFC and Harris 583. He has worked for 20 years in automotive book publishing and is currently publisher with Motorbooks International in the USA.

Acknowledgements

Laverda motorcycles undeniably enjoy cult status within the bike fraternity. A deeply committed band of enthusiasts are dedicated to owning, preserving and, most importantly of all, riding the products of the Breganze factory. I therefore find it bewildering that, thus far, there has been next to nothing in print – even in Italy – to record the trials and achievements of the family company.

This book is intended to right that wrong, by providing a review of the distinctive machines that have emerged from Breganze over the last 40 years. I do not doubt, however, that there are further Laverda tales to tell, that simply cannot be catered for within these pages. If this general history both plugs the yawning gap and inspires others to delve further into the as yet untapped detail, I shall be satisfied.

In seeking information I was particularly fortunate to have been assisted by the energetic British-based International Laverda Owners Club who produce a first-rate club magazine and organise numerous events to fly the Laverda flag.

My particular thanks go to Club members Tim Isles – one of the foremost authorities on the SF/SFC range – for his contribution to Chapter 4, and Phil Todd for kindly writing a couple of road tests.

I should also mention Geoff Rushton for his assistance with background information, and Fernando Bruscoli and Gianni Perrone for their help in digging out photographs, and their unrivalled generosity in so many ways as I have toured Italy. For the provision of detailed inside knowledge of the factory's racing exploits, I thank both Flavio Montesi and Primo Zanzani.

At the Laverda factory, my gratitude goes to Paolo Bauducco and Claudio Beck. But perhaps most importantly I must acknowledge the unstinting assistance and hospitality of Massimo Laverda who scoured his memory to provide the answers to numerous questions. Without Massimo's cooperation I doubt whether this book could have appeared.

For the provision of photographs to illustrate the text, I must record my thanks to the Italian magazines *Moto Capital*, *In Moto* and *La Moto*, together with Ray Sheepwash of the Owners Club.

The Laverda marque will be forever associated in England with the Slater brothers, Roger and Richard. I am delighted that Richard Slater kindly agreed to write the Foreword – there could be no more appropriate person to have done so.

Finally, for her patience as I have consistently disappeared into my study or taken myself off to Italy, thanks to my wife Elizabeth.

Raymond Ainscoe

I should like to reiterate Raymond's thanks; and because my own contribution to the book and experience of Laverda have been different, to add others to the list. Raymond is a student of the Italian motorcycle, an excellent researcher and a most practised writer, having been published many times before. He is intrigued by Moto Laverda. I am, I confess, infatuated. How can I write a short acknowledgement to all the people who have aided and abetted me in this passion since 1974? Somehow I must.

In nearly seventeen years I have undertaken correspondence with hundreds of people, received literally thousands of photographs, followed innumerable leads to a greater understanding of the what, when, how and why of these motorcycles. Luck, and making the most of that luck, has enabled me to visit Breganze on twenty or so occasions. I have interviewed every factory personality, importer, exporter, mechanic, racer, enthusiast and engineer I could find.

Let me thank my wife. Then Massimo Laverda, a good friend, and his wife. Piero Laverda, Hans Blomqvist, Roger and Richard Slater, Uwe Witt, Larry Strung – all friends. Let me thank all those people who have helped me. I hope to use all their contributions some time soon, if not here perhaps in another book.

Tim Parker

75cc Laverda Sport in Milano–Taranto race trim and colours. (*In Moto*)

Foreword

Having been asked by the authors of this superb work to express briefly my thoughts and feelings for Laverda motorcycles, and the cult that has come to surround them, I would say first of all, that the very nature of them was bound to create their well-deserved 'cult' image.

The first 750cc twin, launched two decades ago, was years ahead of its time. Handbuilt by artisans and created by the brothers Massimo and Piero (both passionately enthusiastic motorcyclists) the energy and enthusiasm generated by the project tended to attract like-minded importers and customers. Enthusiasm and dedication to the product were the key factors. The unsurpassed quality of the engineering, allied to that classic Italian design flair, virtually guaranteed a success story from the very beginning of the factory's entry into the big bike market.

There was another vital aspect to the story: the achievements in racing of both the factory and the private teams (such as our own) which competed throughout the seventies, played a crucial role in establishing the name Laverda worldwide.

One model stood out at this point, which helped establish the legend, and really did become one itself: Jota. Synonymous with Laverda, the Jota was created in England with the collaboration of the factory, and subsequently built at Breganze for world markets. Certainly the most charismatic of all Laverdas, the Jota led the class for five years in international production racing, piloted by courageous riders whose skills were necessary to wrestle the brute power to its limits. Even now they are remembered, and revered, as they were a decade ago. It is the same red-blooded, egotistical enthusiast that buys a Jota today. I feel that this machine will enter, in fact has entered, the history books as one of the most successful, awe-inspiring classic Italian motorcycles ever to be produced; and with the proliferating noise and emission legislation, its like will never be produced again.

Whatever model today's Laverda owner rides, be it an SFC750/1000, a Jota, Montjuic, Mirage or Corsa, he is typified as a staunch individualist, who never follows the crowd. Indeed, if he had spent less money he could have bought the latest model from Japan, probably 20% smaller, lighter and faster, but had he done so, he would not have become a part of the great Laverda family.

Richard Slater

Origins

Nestling in the foothills of the scenic Dolomites in the north-eastern corner of the Italian peninsula lies an almost unknown hamlet called Laverda. To the Latin scholar, the village's name provides a tenuous clue to its origins: in Roman times centurions were encamped at the site, using it as a look-out post. Its unimaginative Roman name, 'guardia' or guard post, became with the passage of time 'la ward' and finally Lavarda, or Laverda.

The hamlet in turn gave its name not only to a river (or more accurately an overgrown brook) that ran to the plains to the south but also to some of its inhabitants. In the eighteenth century, one branch of the Laverda family moved a few kilometres south to another village called Breganze, just to the west of the more sizeable town of Bassano del Grappa that owes its enduring celebrity to the universal popularity of the locally produced potent spirit: grappa.

Breganze was, and indeed remains, a sleepy village, with its campanile, the bell-tower, the symbol of Italian civic pride, and not too much else of note. But in the late nineteenth century, at the height of the Italian industrial revolution, the surrounding area could perhaps have been described as an equivalent of Lancashire in England some years before. It was at the forefront of developments in textile and agricultural machinery. Indeed, many of the local entrepreneurs journeyed to England to poach the latest ideas.

One such adventurous spirit was Pietro Laverda of Breganze. He had been a technical assistant in the Institute of Physics at the ancient and highly respected University of Padua but, on the death of his father, he was obliged to return home to support his family. It was there in 1873 that he founded Ditta Pietro Laverda, a firm which initially made small agricultural machinery such as wine and olive presses.

From these humble beginnings the Laverda company was to grow steadily until by the 1970s it was Italy's major manufacturer of agricultural machinery, specialising in combine harvesters and employing about 1,500 workers. The original agricultural machinery factory remains near the centre of Breganze but as an adjunct to the new premises on the edge of town. In 1978 the 'agricultura' was sold by the family shareholders to one of its outside investors, the giant Fiat organisation.

Pietro had two sons, Antonio and Giovanni. The former entered the business at the turn of the century and consolidated its steady growth. Antonio had no fewer than ten children, namly the twins Battista and Piero, Angelina, Elena, Francesco, Giulio, Filiberto, Giorgio, Maria and Bruna, most of whom studied either agriculture or economics with a view to contributing to the family's enterprise. On Antonio's premature death in 1922, the aged Pietro took up the reins again temporarily but they were handed down two generations seven years later when Battista, Piero and Angelina had completed their studies.

1935 was a momentous year for the firm: a new plant was opened, in Breganze once again, producing auxiliary engines designed to be fitted to small farm machinery. It was also in 1935 that a younger brother, Francesco, reluctantly curtailed his research studies in the Faculty of Physics at the University of Padua. After searching his conscience, he was prevailed upon to join his siblings in Breganze, for his appears to have been the most imaginative, innovative and fertile mind within the family.

Henceforth Francesco became the family's leading light, designing much of the required machinery, particularly in the years after the Second World War. Nevertheless, his imagination was not exactly set ablaze by harvesters and he readily turned his hand to other projects. For example, in 1948 he designed and supervised the building of a workers' village in Breganze. The idea was that the construction costs would be met by the Laverda family, that the houses would be occupied by their employees at a modest rent and that shortly thereafter the occupants would be entitled to purchase at discounted prices. Within a few years, the houses were indeed owned by Laverda employees.

Francesco's next project was a motorcycle. Francesco was intrigued by the opportunities for mass production offered by motorcycles and in 1948 he decided to make a four-stroke model in his spare time at home. Making most of the parts by hand in his workshop, within twelve months he had built the first Laverda motorcycle.

He had opted for a 74cc engine, that was slightly inclined forwards, with bore and stroke dimensions of 46×45mm, boasting pushrod operated valves. The engine's construction was all alloy and the barrel had an iron lining. Power output was reputedly 3bhp at 5,200rpm.

OPPOSITE ABOVE An example of the half-dozen first-generation 74cc machines built by Francesco in 1948/1949.

OPPOSITE BELOW The second-generation motorcycle with its elegant egg-shell shaped tank.

LEFT A novel display by a Laverda agent.

ABOVE The factory yard bursting with egg-shells, taken in about 1951.

The Sport version in
its classic form of
the mid-1950s.

ABOVE The development of the egg-shell bike, now featuring a bulkier tank and revised rear suspension.

RIGHT Probably 1952 and Laverda's first approach to what was to become its classic form, with tubular frame, albeit flimsy at this stage. . .[see over]

TOP Yet another version of the second phase 75cc machine (post dating those shown below) – now looking like a genuine motorcycle.

ABOVE LEFT . . . and note the introduction of the updated rear springing and front forks.

LEFT The production line in the tiny factory in the heart of Breganze.

ABOVE A band of marque enthusiasts, riding through Breganze – two up in some cases.

The pressed steel cradle frame was perverse in that it ran alongside rather than below the engine-gearbox unit, and it carried simple pressed steel front forks with a single central spring that was Francesco's sole concession to suspension.

The three-speed gearbox was operated by a rocking pedal on the right hand side. Other features of this prototype were the exhaust pipe running on the right hand side, the bicycle type saddle, the rudimentary lighting system and the 17-inch and 18-inch wheels at the front and rear respectively. The machine was used by its creator as his personal transport and he claimed, perhaps optimistically, a top speed of 45 mph.

At the insistent bidding of his cronies Francesco built five replicas during 1949, although he had to call on the assistance of some of the workers in the agricultural factory for such a grandiose project. All five replicas featured a cast alloy fully enclosed chaincase on the left hand side, reputedly because one customer was the local priest who was concerned lest his cassock should become ensnared in the chain.

Those six humble machines represented the first generation Laverda motorcycle and one of their number is on permanent display in the factory's entrance hall. Their success prompted Francesco to incorporate another company, Moto Laverda SpA, to exploit a niche in the market.

Post-war Italy was crying out for lightweight motorcycles and hordes had appeared virtually overnight. For instance, in 1946 Garelli had launched their hugely successful 38cc Mosquito as an auxiliary engine that could be clipped onto a bicycle and Garelli shortly afterwards produced a complete machine.

A feature of the developments of modern industrial Italy was that new factories were often sited on the edges of towns but the working classes remained in their traditional town centre homes. This, combined with the impoverished public transport system, and the scarcity of petrol, created a vast unsatisfied demand for cheap run-abouts. Francesco saw the opportunity and seized it.

In 1950, a serious production run began. But beforehand the bike underwent a transformation and the second generation Laverda was born. A new pressed

Sports models on show, exhaust pipe switched back to the right for 1952.

ABOVE LEFT **Agents cashed in on the marque's racing successes; note the modified bikes intended for competition use.**

LEFT **A Laverda stand plugging the factory's success in the 1953 Giro d'Italia ...and (ABOVE) the same showboating four years later.**

steel frame was introduced. It was a beam type, akin to that made famous by the NSU Max, with the beam supporting the engine and then extending upwards and rearwards to support the seat and form the rear mudguard.

Nor did the changes stop there. The exhaust pipe was switched to the left, the chain to the right, and the fuel tank was an elegant egg-shaped affair. Like its predecessor, one of these models can be found on display in the factory.

The machine undeniably met its designer's requirements, offering an impressive 200 miles to the gallon. In the first year of production a mere 250 were crafted.

For 1951, a number of refinements were available. It was possible to buy a model that sported telescopic forks and a combined leg-shield-cum-engine-cover that

was intended to appeal to the commuting office worker, anxious to keep the grime of the streets off his trousers.

Perversely, another variant retained the pressed-steel front forks and yet featured a hand-adjustable friction damping for the rear suspension. The pressed-steel frame of this model was also re-designed so that, hand in hand with a bulkier tank, the overall impression was of a much beefier motorcycle.

By 1952, the bike was in its third generation, a style that it was to retain until the end of its production run. This machine was marked by the use of a traditional duplex tubular cradle frame with telescopic front forks and a conventional rear suspension relying on twin spring units, while once again the exhaust pipe was switched, this time back to the right. In appearance, this met the norms of the classic Italian lightweight model of the 1950s, particularly with its eye-catching red and ivory paintwork. Over the years there were refinements to the mudguards, the tank and the saddle that came with or without a pillion and sometimes in elongated form. But essentially the 75cc machine remained untouched henceforth.

From 1953 it was joined by a 100cc version that was obtained by enlarging the bore and stroke to 52mm and 47mm respectively for an actual displacement of 98cc. Both models came in Turismo and Sport forms that

RIGHT Laverda's publicity machine now boasts of the commuter bike that wins races!

BELOW Sporting repute was the lifeblood of Italian marques in the 1950s, and Laverda was able to boast of gold medal success in the 1956 ISDT at Garmisch – note the duly equipped bike to the left of the display.

were generally available to the public, together with a limited run of M-T, or Milano-Taranto, versions designed for competition use.

By 1954, the 75cc Sport version had acquired its definitive guise. Measuring 46 × 45mm, the engine was still slightly inclined forwards and featured a barrel and head in light alloy. A flywheel generator supplied current to an external coil, with a contact breaker mounted on the left hand side of the camshaft. A two pint oil reservoir was integral with the crankcase which incorporated the three-speed gearbox. Also employed were a 16mm Dell'Orto carburettor, 150mm drum brakes and a puny horn on the front downtubes. The tyres were 2.375 × 20in, both front and rear.

The Sport's version other statistics were 4.7bhp at 7,500rpm, sufficient to propel the 150 lb machine to a top speed of 55 mph (as against the Turismo's more modest 3.7bhp at 6,700rpm producing 40 mph). The reported top speed was available, provided that the rider was prone on the tank; if he sat up, a contemporary road test indicated that the speed fell by 4 mph.

Spurred on by the racing successes garnered by the M-T models, sales throughout the decade were encouraging, although less than spectacular. The annual production figures, for the 75cc and 100cc machines combined, were as follows, for a total of 38,455 units. In retrospect this would be Laverda's most prolific model by far.

1949: 5	1954: 9,000
1950: 250	1955: 7,000
1951: 1,500	1956: 6,000
1952: 3,500	1957: 3,000
1953: 8,000	1958: 200

By the mid-1950s the firm was employing over 200 workers, thus making it one of the pre-eminent companies in the Italian motorcycle market.

At this point, well established and in a healthy financial position, Francesco turned his back on the last decade and, prompted by the ambitions of his right hand man Luciano Zen, sought fresh challenges in another sector of the market.

Riding a Laverda 100: Tim Parker

I bought a 1957 Laverda 100 Turismo, 3-speed with the half-width alloy hubs, dual seat but still low bars. Its mudguards pretend to be valanced. Its colour was maroon with some ivory. To its great benefit it is both a proper motorcyle and lightweight at the same time. By this I mean that compared with, say, a BSA Bantam it feels complete, as though it has some strength, yet without undue mass. It has integrity.

It is well engineered and well made, an expression one hears a great deal when discussing Laverda motorcycles. Of course it uses many proprietary components then available from the large Italian industry but they are well matched. 100cc is not a large displacement by any measure, yet it does not feel slow or over-stretched as one rides along. I think this suggests good balance. It starts, idles and shifts into gear smoothly. It is easy to ride. The engine is jewel-like with a not dissimilar feel to the overhead cam Honda singles of a few years later. And it is frugal. Like many an Italian economy bike of the era it has longevity far in excess of its price. Again like those early Hondas, the Laverda 100 lasts. Maybe 'Four started, Four finished' was not such an inappropriate sales slogan (see p. 28).

My 100 awaits restoration. Innumerable miles, a dozen owners recorded, yet all it really needs is the wheels to be re-spoked, new sprockets, steering head bearings, some oil seals replacing and top-end overhaul. Running maintenance rather than actual restoration, perhaps?

Co-author Tim Parker's 1957 100 Turismo as delivered from Bassano del Grappa to Hammersmith, London, in 1985. Only mild restoration is necessary. Unoriginal are the silencer, the seat and the addition of the luggage rack. Seat and silencer can be found or made. This is three speed with single-sided, slim wheel hubs. (Tim Parker)

Laverda 100: Raymond Ainscoe

My Laverda Turismo, also a 100 (or more properly a 98cc), is actually a 1958 model. There is little to differentiate it from its predecessor apart from its four-speed gearbox, its full-width hubs and the option of high bars. It is finished in a dark blue that, despite initial scepticism, was discovered to be an original works colour from the late 1950s.

I was attracted to the machine for its UK rarity value; I doubt whether there are more than two in the country. When I bought it, the Laverda had just undergone a partial restoration, courtesy of marque fans Tim and Dave, the brothers Isles. Although complete, it had not yet fired but Tim assured me that there would be no problems. True enough, once home, the battery was charged, petrol poured in, a kick administered and the tiny engine instantly burst into very healthy sounding life.

The handsome twins and triples of the 1970s are bywords for solid engineering, but the foundations of this reputation were clearly laid with this 98cc motor and its 74cc sibling.

Admittedly, the rider of my particular machine might struggle to surpass 35 mph, and that downhill with the wind behind him – and whether the extra gear was really necessary is open to debate. But it is possible to appreciate how it was that these tiny engines were regarded by the works riders of the day as 'unburstable' during the Giro d'Italia and Milano-Taranto. Ever heard the story of the tortoise and the hare?

Raymond Ainscoe's 1958 four-speed 100cc machine – still a handy commuter thirty years on. The engine (ABOVE) is neat, simple and elegant looking – not to mention reliable and good for the Milano-Taranto.

Racing in the 1950s

Although the ultra-lightweight Laverdas were never unequivocally at the forefront of the sporting stage, the marque's racing endeavours and achievements during the 1950s certainly merit a mention.

If the sole international participation of any permanent note was the acquisition of three gold medals in the 100cc class of the ISDT at Garmisch-Partenkirschen in 1956, nevertheless it is fair to claim that the tiddlers from Breganze were significant contributors to the domestic racing scene for the best part of the decade.

As early as 1950 Francesco optimistically entered a 75cc machine in the classic Milano-Taranto epic. This was a single-stage open roads marathon that dated back to 1919 when, known as the Raid Nord-Sud, the inaugural event was won by Ettore Girardi aboard his 350cc split single two-stroke Garelli. In those far-off days the pioneer riders finished their trek at Naples but in time the event was extended to Taranto in the heel of Italy. During the 1930s it was tactfully dubbed the Mussolini Cup in honour of Il Duce who was a confirmed motorcycling fantatic.

On its revival after the War, the Milano-Taranto remained hugely popular with the Italian factories and indeed their star riders, and crucially with the enthusiastic spectators who thronged the route. Of course, they were potential purchasers and in that fact lay the *raison d'être* of the participation of many of the works teams.

Upwards of 300 riders would leave Milan in the dead of night astride machines of all types and sizes from flimsy looking 75cc sports models to fully-fledged GP racers, duly fitted with lighting equipment. Indeed, in 1955 Bruno Francisci won the race aboard a four cylinder 500cc Gilera that was in exactly the same state of tune as Geoff Duke's TT-winning version, victorious just a few days beforehand. After what was perhaps the ultimate test of endurance, some 900 miles later, depending on the particular route that varied from year to year, maybe a third of the starters would eventually wend their weary way into Taranto.

In the marque's experimental foray the singleton Laverda failed at Rome but in 1951 four machines were entered and all finished safe and sound. Cashing in on the potential for publicity, Francesco coined the somewhat unimaginative advertising slogan: 'Four left, four arrived'.

In those years, most Italian manufacturers opted for two-stroke power plants for their ultra-lightweight machines but Francesco appreciated that the reliability of four-stroke engines should have given them the edge in long-distance events. Unfortunately for him, the Capriolo concern in Trento – a division of the Caproni aircraft company – simultaneously came to the same conclusion. It was the Capriolo four-stroke – that bore a striking resemblance to Francesco's first machine of 1948/49 – that took the chequered flag as the class winner.

But from then on, Laverda's 75cc Milano-Taranto – the 'racing' machine was so dubbed – came into its own, virtually monopolising its class with Castellani taking the laurels in 1952 at a speed of 47.47 mph. In the following year, the first 14 places were occupied by Laverdas led home by Fontanili's model. The run of success was punctuated by Claudio Galliani's victory for rivals Capriolo in 1954 but Larquier and Pastorelli re-established the *status quo* in the two events run thereafter.

Indeed, with the introduction of the 98cc M-T model, 100cc class victories were registered in 1954 and 1956 thanks to Larquier and Marchi respectively, the latter at an average speed of no less than 58.59 mph.

In truth, these modest racing steeds differed little from the tubular framed sports model. Francesco provided the M-T racers with a high compression piston, a revised head and an option of primary drive by either chain or gear. A larger Dell'Orto carburettor, an 18mm version, was fitted and a four-speed gearbox was incorporated. The tyres were also slightly fatter than those on the roadsters, measuring 2.50 by 20in.

Francesco claimed 10bhp at 13,000rpm for the competitive M-T speedster, but there are undoubtedly lies, damned lies, statistics and bhp claims. More realistic figures to emerge were 7bhp at 9,600rpm for the 75cc version and 8.5bhp at 9,000rpm for its larger brother. Top speed for the models was of the order of 75 mph and 80 mph. Even in those days the marque had gained a reputation for the strength of its engines. In the Milano-Taranto, there was a stretch of road, measuring some 200 miles, along which it was possible to keep the tiny Laverdas on full throttle throughout.

Flavio Montesi riding to a Gold Medal, 1956 ISDT.

MONTESI FLAVIO - MEDAGLIA D'ORO 6 GIORNI 1956

TROFEO - CEO - GIANFERARI

OPPOSITE **By 1950 Francesco was entering his egg-shell tanked 75cc machine in local competitions, with a small team of three or four riders, here photographed (OPPOSITE BELOW) in readiness for a rally based around the Dolomites.**

ABOVE **Rally participation duly led to some small publicity value when the machines were displayed by an agent based in nearby Trento.**

LEFT **Before the tubular framed bike came into its own, the pressed steel precursor was campaigned, complete with makeshift tank cushions.**

One of the team riders, Flavio Montesi, actually had the confidence to test his bike in this manner, reporting that 'it never missed a beat'.

In 1953 began Laverda's glorious association with the revived Giro d'Italia, or Lap (or Tour) of Italy. The original Giro of the 1920s had been a long-distance inter-city race which had attracted the star names of the day such as Achille Varzi and Tazio Nuvolari but the Giro is undoubtedly best remembered for the series of five races held in the mid-1950s.

Unlike the non-stop Milano-Taranto, the Moto Giro took place in stages over half a dozen days or so, each stage covering more than 200 miles, and the machines, which were essentially sports production bikes, could not exceed 175cc. The inaugural event, inspired by the respected journalist De Deo Ceccarelli and sponsored by his employer, Bologna's daily sports paper *Stadio*,

LEFT The pressed steel framed bike and someone imagining that he is Umberto Masetti ....

BELOW LEFT Dario Widmann, Laverda's man in Trento, advertises his wares.

BELOW An example of the unsophisticated nature of the back-up available to the team during the long distance raids... with a bike casually strapped to a roof rack.

started and finished in Bologna, and an unexpected victory fell to a humble 125cc two-stroke, a Benelli Leoncino.

Laverda rider Mariani did however hit *Stadio*'s headlines, being the first 75cc machine home and the factory scooped the team award, the Dragoni Gold Cup. Mariani repeated his success in 1954 but in the next edition longstanding Capriolo opponent Galliani hit the jackpot. 1956 and 1957 saw Laverda back on the podium, with Jacopini and Montesi respectively first past the post in the class.

With the appearance of the 100cc model, Primo Zanzani took a class success in 1954 and enjoyed the satisfaction of humbling the massed ranks of the pushrod Ducati opposition. Alas, the tables were turned in the following year when the Ducati Marianna set a host of new records over the nine stages and pushed every Laverda entrant into retirement. The victories of Marchi and Pastorelli did however redress the balance and restore some pride in 1956 and 1957.

The 1957 Moto Giro was held just a few days before the final, tragic Mille Miglia. When de Portago's Ferrari careered into a crowd, killing its driver, passenger and thirteen spectators, the curtain fell on the anachronism that was open-road racing in Italy. The days of the 'Terrible Twins', the Milano-Taranto and the Giro, were over – at least until their revival in rally format at the end of the 1980s, as part of the classic motorcycling renaissance that swept the peninsula.

Laverda riders at the start of a stage in the 1954 *Giro d'Italia* (Tour of Italy).

ABOVE Flavio Montesi taking the chequered flag in the final edition of the Milano-Taranto, 1956.

BELOW Team riders Silvagni, Rippa and Jacopini during the Moto Giro, 1956.

RIGHT Mariani, Montesi and Galliani photographed during a Giro – the vests advertise the *Stadio*, the daily sports paper that sponsored the event.

The Laverda squad
at the start of a stage
of the Giro; Flavio
Montesi wears
number 30.

JACOPINI BRUNO VINCITORE MOTOGIRO CLASSE 75 CC

LEFT **Jacopini, victorious in the 75cc class of the Moto Giro, 1956.**

ABOVE **Flavio Montesi ready for the next 200-mile stage of the Giro.**

SILVAGNI - CAMPIONE ITALIANO CLASSE 75 CC.
MARCHI - VINCITORE MOTOGIRO E MILANO-TARANTO 1956 CLASSE 100 CC. D. S.

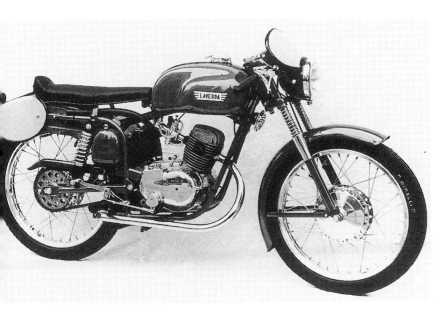

OPPOSITE ABOVE Laverda teamsters Genunzio Silvagni (left) and Marchi won junior championships in 1956 and 1957 on a 75cc machine, fairly uncommon track successes to put alongside the Laverda endurance victories.

OPPOSITE. BELOW Montesi hustles a 100cc machine to victory at Vallelunga, beating Silvio Grassetti's works 125cc Benelli in the process.

THIS PAGE Sports machines in various states of modification for competition use.

Although the Laverda tiddlers will be forever associated with those energy-sapping tests of endurance, a limited number of track successes were also registered. The most notable of these were perhaps Genunzio Silvagni's junior championships in 1956 and 1957 aboard a 75cc machine fettled by Zanzani. In 1956, he raced in the Modified Sports category which the FMI, the Italian equivalent of the ACU, recast as Formula 2 for the following season. In effect, this category catered for racers derived from sports production machines, not unlike the modern day TT Formula. Silvagni's racer was a thinly-disguised M-T model, featuring nominal tweaks such as a revised exhaust pipe, a larger front drum brake, modified mudguards and the like.

One of the foremost Laverda riders of these times was Primo Zanzani. Born in Forli in 1923, after the war he worked at Forli airport on the ubiquitous Caproni aeroplanes, while he cut his racing teeth aboard a 125cc Morini and a modified production Gilera Saturno. It was in 1953 that he first turned to Laverda motorcycles, racing a 75cc version that was prone to engine trouble. His efforts, however, did not go unnoticed and Francesco offered him a works machine for the next season, with which he took the laurels in the 1954 Giro.

Although Zanzani now had 'works' assistance, he emphasised that not too much should be read into this: 'You must remember that at that time Laverda was not really a factory in today's sense; it was really little more than an enlarged workshop. And when the team rode in the Giro, it was still essentially a private effort. Laverda provided a machine and two or three mechanics and that was it. For winning my class in the Giro I won the princely sum of 25,000 lire – about £10 – but fortunately Laverda covered our expenses so at least we weren't out of pocket.'

Zanzani retired from the tracks at the end of the 1957 season and began a career as chief engineer with the Motobi concern of Pesaro, before moving on to fulfil a similar role with Benelli when the two factories merged in the early 1960s.

With the termination of open-roads racing, Laverda's official participation in the sport was suspended for a dozen years but, in private hands, the Breganze tiddlers continued to roam the tracks. Between 1959 and 1964, no fewer than seven national titles, both track and mountain climbing, fell to the marque. Of these, probably the most prestigious fell to Pietro Mencaglia who appropriated the 1960 100cc F2 championship. When, four years later, Mencaglia added the 75cc mountain title to his collection, so impressed was Francesco that he presented a 75cc M-1 bike to him as a mark of his appreciation.

LEFT At the start of a stage of the 1990 Giro d'Italia, Gaetano Pasqualini readies himself and his 1954 Laverda Milano-Taranto model, while ex-MV Agusta star Emilio Mendogni prepares his 125cc Morini. (Raymond Ainscoe)

ABOVE Close up of the immaculate 75cc machine as it sets off on another trek of 200 miles, a quarter of a century after it did it for real. (Raymond Ainscoe)

CHAPTER 3

The early 1960s

Even the dedicated Laverda buff has to admit that the products of the Breganze factory during the first years of the 1960s did little to consolidate the marque's reputation.

In the late 1950s, the bubble that was the buoyant Italian motorcycle industry undoubtedly burst. Primarily this was because of the ready availability of modestly priced cars, typified by the Fiat 5009 and 6009 models. Their appearance meant that the erstwhile bike owner could suddenly afford to – and did – purchase an economical car in which he could both commute and transport his family in some comfort during his leisure hours.

The most obvious sign of the impending problem was the unexpected withdrawal from the international race tracks of the Moto Guzzi, Mondial and Gilera squads at the end of 1957, as escalating costs began to bite. Within a few years, famous and long-established names were ignominiously to bite the dust, such as Bianchi, while others, like Gilera, staggered from one financial crisis to another.

To survive, Laverda obviously had to change course and the route chosen henceforth was largely dictated by Francesco's character. His son, Massimo, explained Francesco's priorities thus: 'My father was never really a motorcycle enthusiast; it was never his hobby. But he was a moral man, with a social conscience, and his constant concern was to build economical machines for the working classes, who were still relatively badly off. Accordingly, the new machines of the 1960s all had one feature in common: excellent fuel consumption.'

Francesco was aided throughout by the company's first employee, Luciano Zen. Zen was no trained engineer, and far less an inspired guru in the Carcano or Taglioni mould, but he was a loyal component and, almost by default, he was the company's *de facto* chief designer.

Zen's panacea for the factory's perceived ills was to step sideways, and he intended to tap the scooter niche already exploited with such success by Lambretta and Vespa. He chose a hard nut to crack, for both the market leaders, with production dating back to 1946, had established worldwide reputations that had been enhanced by an extravaganza of record-breaking sessions in the early 1950s. Crucially, they enjoyed the back-up of the substantial Innocenti and Piaggio concerns respectively. The harsh truth was that Lav-

erda was entering this particular market place a dozen years too late.

Scooterettes – 50cc two-stroke engines under scooter bodies – were increasingly popular and within a few years respected companies such as Agrati and Motobi were to dip their corporate toes into these waters. In keeping with this trend, Zen's first effort was a two-speed 50cc affair which went into production in 1959. However, the Laverda engine was a four-stroke!

The tiny pushrod 48.9cc engine, with bore and stroke measurements of 40×39mm, featured a light alloy cylinder and head with a cast iron barrel. Other details were flywheel magneto ignition, a one gallon tank, a tiny Dell'Orto SH carburettor, single seat and 2.75×9in. tyres. The motor's 2.5bhp at 6,000rpm powered a dwarf of a 139 lb machine to a top speed reputedly in excess of 30 mph.

Within a year, a slightly larger version appeared, boasting three speeds and a 47mm stroke that took displacement to 59cc. The 3bhp available boosted top speed to 40 mph and offered the luxury of a dual seat. As Francesco had insisted, undoubtedly the most noteworthy feature of these models was their phenomenal fuel economy, prompting the sales blurb to claim 180mpg.

It was at this stage that Francesco's son Massimo, arguably just as pivotal to the marque's legendary status as his father, stepped onto the stage. Massimo, by both nature and intellect, was much given to the classics and philosophy that he had studied at the University of Padua. Nevertheless, he had the wit to appreciate that, being a Laverda, his true vocation was inevitably that of an engineer. He took up the story: 'After a couple of years at university I told my father that it was time I started work. However, I had had no formal engineering background and so my father packed me off to Modena for eighteen months or so to gain some practical experience with Ferrari and Maserati. And so, although I had no engineering training, I knew what I was doing and could speak the language of engineering.'

Early in 1961, Francesco managed to sell some of his scooters to Eric Sulley, who later achieved some repute with Honda in the UK, but who was at that time managing director of Scootamatic Limited. For pro-

50cc scooters lined up in the factory.

OPPOSITE **Francesco Laverda extols the virtues of a 50cc mini-scooter.**

LEFT **60cc scooter, still with some original tassles on the dual seat, photographed just outside the factory in 1984. It is believed that employees were offered the slow selling models at advantageous prices. (Tim Parker)**

motion purposes, Massimo and factory tester and racer Lino Marchi set off from Breganze and at a steady 25 mph rode 920 miles through Germany and Belgium to meet Francesco beneath London's Big Ben in a blaze of contrived publicity. Contrived because in fact the intrepid duo had arrived in London some twelve hours ahead of schedule and so had an extra night wallowing in the luxury of the Savoy Hotel. Next morning, when lining up for the obligatory photographs in Westminster, Massimo's newly washed clean-shaven face seemed ill-becoming such an adventure and so he duly rubbed his hands against a soot-laden tree and transferred some of the muck onto his face.

A grand reception and press conference was then held in the Savoy, no doubt totally overshadowing a reception attended by Princess Margaret in the adjoining room. Mr J L Turner, the Chairman of Scootamatic, proudly announced that each machine had completed the journey on fewer than six gallons at a cost of under £2 – those really were the days!

In an effort to glean even more publicity, Mr Turner than presented a scooter to the student midwives at Lewisham hospital; they were evidently deemed to be worthy and needy recipients of such an economical means of transport. The whole saga was duly recorded for posterity by the cameras of Movietone News and indeed shown in hundreds of cinemas across the land.

Sadly, despite these public relations initiatives the scooters never really caught on. Production lasted a mere two years, although the left-overs were still being sold off some years later. Montesa in Barcelona bought a licence to produce the 60cc scooter to salvage some of the investment.

Hand-in-hand with the scooters, the Breganze offerings included a couple of totally uninspiring mopeds to which the ardent marque diehard may wish to apply the Nelsonian technique of turning a blind eye. First of all, in 1959 came a 49cc model called the Laverdino which boasted a slightly inclined pushrod engine with a three-speed gearbox beneath a backbone-type frame with traditional front telescopic and rear swinging arm suspension, skimpy drum brakes and a tiny tank. The overall package was anything but a thing of beauty. Predictably it failed to sell in bulk, although astonishingly, production lingered on for five years.

In 1964 its replacement stepped onto the stage: a stark two-stroke moped. The frame was simplicity itself: one tube running from the steering head diagonally down to the pressed steel rear fork section. Slung beneath this was the 47.8cc cylinder which produced 1.5bhp at 4,200rpm. There was a 3-litre fuel tank, a 5% petroil mix, flywheel magneto ignition and an automatic clutch.

An unusual feature, stopping the 24×1.75in. wheels, was the use of cable-operated disc brakes, which Laverda claimed as a 'first' in Italy on a production machine. The top speed of 25 mph was certainly miserable but the machine's puny weight, a paltry 70 lb, contributed to its quite exceptional fuel economy: well in excess of 200mpg.

Laverda's over-optimistic sales handouts boasted that these models sold in great numbers throughout

Italy. Alas, the production figures reveal the disappointing truth; 2,300 in 1964 and 2,750 in the following year; hardly sufficient to found a dynasty!

No, forget the humble mini-scooters and the unexciting mopeds, for the hopes of the factory in these years rested with the 200cc twin cylinder machine that was launched at the Milan Show in November 1961. *Motor Cycling*'s Italian correspondent, the arch-enthusiast Giovanni Luraschi, did give Laverda credit for being 'the only manufacturer prepared to launch something really new ... with a 200cc parallel twin four-stroke machine developed from the famous 75cc and 100cc singles.' Luraschi reported that the new twin shared the

stand with the 50cc mini-scooter as the other models in the range had been dropped, which move he assessed as logical enough on the grounds that a 200 would have greater appeal than a 75 or a 100 to the type of customer not beguiled by the *ciclomotori* and the scooters.

The engine of the new model was nothing startling, in essence a doubled-up version of the 52 × 47mm ohv motor, thereby attaining 199.5cc, with 18bhp on offer at 6,500rpm. Features were flywheel magneto ignition, a Dell'Orto carburettor, a 2-litre wet sump and a four-speed gearbox.

The frame was essentially tubular, with twin downtubes at the front, but the rear was a pressed steel affair

OPPOSITE Laverdinos, Lusso to the left and Turismo to the right.

ABOVE A Laverdino Turismo can be seen on the far left of this showroom display.

LEFT A Laverda 2-stroke moped; to the left is a Laverdino Turismo. Both were in daily use by two of the workforce at the Laverda factory in 1984. Neither have needed restoration for 20 years. The moped usually carried a large screen and flexible leg shields. Metal leg shields can be seen on the Laverdino. (Tim Parker)

of which an extension became the mudguard, in turn supporting a dual seat. Springing was conventional: telescopics at the front and a swinging fork at the rear with Ceriani suspension units. The tyres, 3 × 17in, were Pirelli. Initially, two colour schemes were available: red/black and green/black, but a blue option was soon on offer.

Soon after the launch, the machine was road-tested by *Motociclismo*'s then fledgling reporter Carlo Perelli, subsequently its stalwart deputy editor. The first point he noted was that although the brake pedal was on the right, and the gear change on the left, which was contrary to the usual Italian set-up, nevertheless there was no difficulty as the pedals were well placed as were the handlebar controls. These features, together with what Perelli described as 'stability and handling that would be the envy of any sports motorcycle', contributed to a very comfortable ride.

The tester was particularly complimentary about the clutch and gearbox, with changes being sweet and silent and the gears well spaced. The motor was responsive and indeed, whereas the factory had claimed a top speed of 68 mph, Perelli coaxed 73 mph out of the twin during a test at Monza, albeit flat on the tank and possibly with the wind behind him.

Perelli was equally impressed with the large full-width drum brakes that had been designed for the last of the singles. He reported that the braking action was nicely progressive and energetic without being brutal. As with its stable mates, the twin's fuel economy was a plus factor. Without a passenger, touring at a modest 40 mph, 25 mpg was available, but even two up at 45 mph offered a more than respectable 100mpg.

The machine's lack of vibration and engine noise was also particularly notable, aided no doubt by the rubber blocks placed between the engine and the frame.

Motociclismo's test report concluded with the handsome comment that 'the 200cc twin has three principal qualities: economical to run, good looks and robustness. It is sold at a price a little below an ultra-lightweight sportster and we can recommend it not only to keen motorcyclists who for some time have been waiting for such a machine from our domestic industry but also to those who need a modern middleweight machine whether for work or pleasure.' The twin sold moderately well in Italy. A few were exported, some into the USA, no less, under the name 'Gemini'.

The next machine to emerge from the Breganze stable, at the Milan Show at the tail end of 1965, was the 125cc Sport. The prototype was developed over the next six months and flogged to death by chief factory tester Rizzitelli and his cohorts. Before the machine and its companion, the Trail, went into final production, Massimo (now increasingly involved in design and planning) offered them to *Motociclismo* for extensive tests. He was fearful that the factory testers were adapting themselves to the defects of the machines and

A moped that's obviously done enough for a pension photographed outside the factory in 1989, still in constant use, with leg shields and screen. (Raymond Ainscoe)

thus missing the obvious.

Hence, the Sport was consigned to the mercies of the magazine's young reporter, Roberto Patrignani, who already had a wealth of long distance open roads and TT experience behind him. Patrignani was given the silver and black prototype to test over 300 miles of mountainous roads to the north of Vicenza.

The aircooled pushrod motor was virtually horizontal and measured 56 × 50mm for 123.15cc and produced 10.5bhp. It featured a light alloy head, a 28mm inlet and a 23mm exhaust valve, set at 30 degrees. It was slung beneath a simple tubular frame with the twin front down tubes dropping to the upper base of the cylinder so that the engine was an integral part of the frame. Other mechanical features were a Dell'Orto UB20BS carburettor, a four-speed gearbox

200cc Twin. Perhaps not sold well enough in the face of competition from Japan but by no means a feeble motorcycle: in reality very quiet and smooth and quite peppy. A nice lightweight motorcycle. (*Cycle World*)

with a pedal on the right, a multiple disc wet clutch, gear primary drive and chain final. The tyres, measuring 2.5 × 17in. at the front and 2.75 × 17in. at the rear, relied on standard 'Italian industry' suspension and full-width drum brakes.

The deep and bulbous-looking tank carried over 11 litres and was lined with rubber knee grips. There was also a spacious compartment underneath the seat carrying the 6 volt battery and tools.

At the conclusion of his exhaustive test, Patrignani weighed in with a host of criticisms. The handlebars, being set too low, put too much strain on the forearms during a lengthy journey, and indeed Laverda had foreseen this difficulty and were to offer touring bars as an alternative.

The kickstart was adjudged ineffective and the heel and toe gear change was berated as being too short for ease of operation and too hard to operate. A final criticism was that, if anything, the suspension was too good, so that the machine felt excessively light and handled like a moped.

On the positive side, the engine was assessed to be one of the best ever tested for its silence and elasticity. Even though the gearing on the test machine was faulty, Patrignani reported that the 195 lb mule accelerated nippily, climbed well and hit the claimed top speed of 72 mph at 8,200rpm – although for this last task he had to lie prone on the tank.

Shortly after the 125cc Sport came into production, an enlarged model was on offer in the USA with bore and stroke increased to 58mm and 56mm respectively for 147.96cc; in other respects it was identical.

As Patrignani tested the Sport, so did his colleague Carlo Perelli try out its sister, the 125cc 'Trail'. This was not the factory's first venture into off-road escapades; previous successes included a gold medal in the ISDT and a national championship in the 1950s, while Massimo was a particular off-road enthusiast, having competed extensively in regional events.

To tap a perceived market, in the Spring of 1966 work had begun on a companion model for the Sport. There were obvious cosmetic touches to set the Trail

OPPOSITE ABOVE **200cc** Twin and Francesco Laverda.

LEFT The Twin and the scooters on display

ABOVE **1966 125cc Sport** at announcement. It is thought that many more Trail models were made than Sports, making the Sport very rare today. The formula was right on paper, at least.

apart – high handlebars, the high skimpy mudguards, upswept exhaust, a smaller tank with larger knee pads, Ceriani moto cross suspension units, with the rear unit enjoying three settings, and a garish yellow and black colour scheme.

The prototypes were put through their paces in the mountainous area to the north of Breganze by Massimo and his right-hand-man Andrea Gatos. Thereafter, one was consigned to Perelli who echoed many of Patrignani's criticisms of the Sport: an antiquated, insecure gear change and an inadequate lock.

The Trail's frame differed from that of its precursor in that halfway along the top tube two new tubes sprouted vertically joining the usual downtubes at the top of the crankcase, providing extra rigidity. The tyres were 2.75 × 17in at the front and 3.25 or 3.50 × 16in at the rear. The smaller tank, containing fewer than 9 litres, meant that the range was reduced to 210 miles.

Again, a 150cc version was soon made available for the transatlantic market. This bike was yet another Laverda to be marketed in the USA under another guise, this time posing first as a Garelli and then as an American Eagle. Again, it never really caught on.

The Trail had been introduced at 270,000 lire but at the Milan Show of 1967 a more sophisticated edition for competition use, the 'Regolarita Corsa', came onto the market at 330,000 lire.

In 1967 Laverda engaged as technical assistant the former Italian trials champion Luigi Gorini who tested the prototype in competition throughout the season, including participation in the severe and prestigious Valli Bergamasche.

November 1966, Laverda's 125 Trail, sometimes called Trail RS. There were numerous versions of this particular model. This looks to be an Italian market version with high front mudguard. Note rocking gear lever, air filter and sump dipstick, which was to survive for another twenty years in virtually the same form. (*Cycle World*)

The most notable variation on the Corsa was that the frame was a complete duplex affair but peculiarly the downtubes ran across the top of the engine instead of below it. Other touches were that the tank, mudguards and numberplates were now plastic. To encourage use of the machine both on the road and in competition, Laverda offered a silencer for the former, in order to enable the rider to avoid the otherwise inevitable fines, and a full technical back-up for the latter.

Again tested by a *Motociclismo* squad, praise was heaped upon the clutch, the lively acceleration and the excellent roadholding provided by the Ceriani units. The major criticisms were levelled at the gear change because the pedal was regarded as overly vulnerable in a fall and a fifth speed in the box was sorely missed.

The harsh truth was that these dowdy unexciting machines were never going to set the motorcycling world ablaze and were never the stuff of legend. Fortunately, and possibly despite, rather than because of, the inclinations of its founder Francesco, the company was about to change its direction.

In defence of the mini-scooter: Tim Parker

A two-speed 50cc four-stroke fan-cooled engine that you sit on, quite literally 'propped up' by a pair of 8-inch wheels that you cannot see, all pretending to be a motorised bicycle, does not sound interesting or safe. Laverda's mini-scooter is both. The shape of the chassis, often in white or pale green, is certainly scooter-like, as say Vespa or Lambretta, and is sweet, if not handsome or classic. Above all, it worked.

Stand astride the machine, turn the key, turn on the fuel and kick. The engine is easy to start and soon to idle. It buzzes a little even though it is actually rubber mounted although it is quite quiet. The 50, at least, featured a large two-part silencer with two tail pipes which exited the chassis either side of the rear wheel.

Pull in the clutch, twist the gear-change wrist for an easy first gear selection. Add revs and as the buzz increases only a fraction more it is ready for take-off. Slow acceleration is unassuming if comfortable and just plain easy. Shifting into second (and top) is equally easy and with some practice can be smooth. Continued travel can be had that simply.

No wobble at under about 25 mph indicated, sedate cornering and capable braking are also available if one remembers that it is 1960 and 50cc. This is not a silly, unusable machine, just one that was mis-targeted, too little, too late. It was a reasonable shot at a shrinking marketplace, a shot many a much larger corporation (which should have known better) could have made (and many did) and failed.

Like most Laverdas, it was well engineered and well made. One should perhaps remember that all successful scooters were actually two-strokes and as with most other forms of personal transport, speed became of the essence. Speed is not something a 50cc (one up) or 60cc (two up) four-stroke scooter can do for you.

Virtually untouched 1960 50cc mini-scooter, one co-author Tim Parker bought and kept in 1982, imported into the UK by Eric Sulley's organisation. The spindly exhaust system is not correct. (Tim Parker)

CHAPTER

750cc twins: GT and GTL, S and SF

There can be little doubt that, in the early 1960s, the Laverda motorcycle company suffered the onset of a potentially terminal illness. Bedevilled for some years from within home shores by four-wheeled competition, it was going nowhere, fast. That the patient rose from its sickbed and within a couple of years was producing motorcycles that two decades later truly merit the tag 'classic', with escalating prices to prove it, is almost entirely due to the vision of one young man, Massimo Laverda.

Massimo Laverda explained the renaissance of his father's company in these terms: 'My first genuine involvement with the design and production of motorcycles was with the 125cc Sport and Trail machines. I was trying to change our philosophy by producing sports machines instead of the utility bikes that my father had always favoured. I was convinced at that time that, as a means of transport, pure and simple, the motorcycle was finished. It could be cold, dirty, wet, uncomfortable; a car was now available to the working classes at an affordable price. Who would buy a motorbike?'

In dealing with that poser, Massimo's own predilections came into play, for he was an out-and-out enthusiast, with a BMW R69S for his everyday transport, which he held in the highest regard for the excellence of its engineering, and a Vincent Black Shadow for fun.

Answering his own question, Massimo was convinced that 'the future of the motorcycle was as a source of recreation and pleasure, a means of sport. I also noticed that the enthusiast does not simply enjoy riding, his pleasure does not stop there. He takes a pride in his machine and enjoys exhibiting it to his friends. Near Breganze there is a winding hillside road and at weekends the local riders would blast up it, park their bikes at the top and then wander round discussing each other's machines. Having bought a bike, a rider would be devastated if his friends did not pile round it to admire its features. He would soon sell it and buy another. I realised that people buy bikes and are interested in them not simply to ride them but to see them, to touch them, to hear them and indeed to smell them.'

Massimo had read about the burgeoning of the hitherto dormant American market and explained the

metamorphosis: 'Until the start of the decade the average American regarded motorcycles with suspicion. They associated them with Harleys, teddy boys, all that sort of image; they were dirty, downmarket, eccentric. But then Honda's marketing policy started to change all that. It was brilliant. They launched thousands of adverts showing respectable, sober, grey-suited businessmen astride their lightweight machines, from 80cc, 125cc to 300cc. They were trying to get through to a potentially vast market, to convince Americans that "normal" people could use motorcycles.'

He decided to go to the Land of the Free to glean some ideas but opted to steer clear of dealers, feeling that they would be blinkered, concerned only with the here and now, whereas Massimo was after a more visionary overview. Therefore before setting off he chatted with Carlo Perelli who gave him a number of introductions to American journalists. Thus forearmed, in 1964 Massimo spent three weeks in California and New York, poaching ideas, trying to foresee future trends.

Massimo outlined the conclusions he came to: 'I spoke to the journalists at *Cycle World* and they were all of the view that the American philosophy of "Bigger is Better" was just about to seep its way into the motorcycle market. They were convinced that within two to three years there would be a great demand for large capacity machines. In turn, it seemed to me that, as in many aspects, Europe would inevitably follow the American lead. I returned home absolutely certain that we should turn our attention to big, sporting bikes. I spent six months trying to convince my father that this was the route we should take, but both he and Zen were against it. It was contrary to everything they had been doing for fifteen years. In truth, I never did convince my father but eventually I wore him down and he agreed to give me full rein.'

So it was that after a gestation period of some 18 months, Laverda's tentative foray into the large capacity market came in 1966: a 654cc, 75 × 74mm, twin-cylinder bike. Very much a surprise exhibit at the Earls Court Show late in the year, the big twin certainly hit the headlines and was destined to be the first of a glorious line of twins and triples from the Breganze factory.

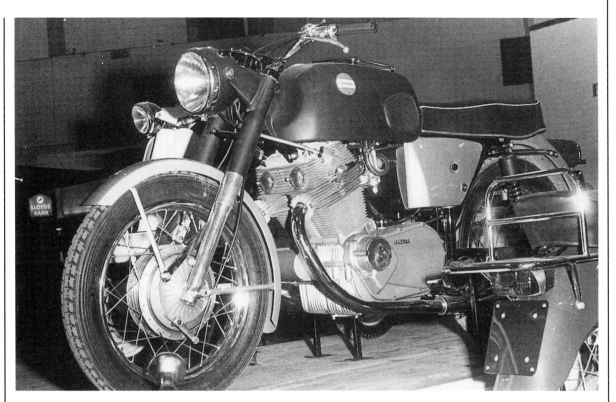

TOP The annual Motorcycle Show at Earls Court, London in November 1966 was chosen for the announcement of the Laverda 650 twin. It almost stole the show! Obviously strong, certainly well made and nicely styled, it was to remain throughout its ten-year life a competitive motorcycle. Nearly 18,500 units were made in total; hardly 100 would be 650s (B. R. 'Nick' Nicholls)

ABOVE A factory promotional shot of the 650. Influences can be seen from Norton, BMW and, of course, Honda. No one has yet to account for the apparent matte paint on the tank. Careful study of the machine reveals that it was well designed from the beginning: little that was fundamental was changed in its production life. Grimeca brakes, Smiths instruments and steel rims.

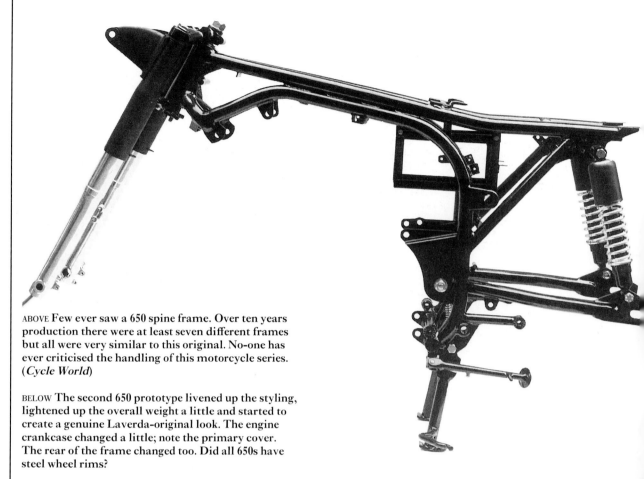

ABOVE Few ever saw a 650 spine frame. Over ten years production there were at least seven different frames but all were very similar to this original. No-one has ever criticised the handling of this motorcycle series. (*Cycle World*)

BELOW The second 650 prototype livened up the styling, lightened up the overall weight a little and started to create a genuine Laverda-original look. The engine crankcase changed a little; note the primary cover. The rear of the frame changed too. Did all 650s have steel wheel rims?

ABOVE The first 750 was a GT model; this one is to US-market specifcation. With an overbore from 650 to 750 the machine picked up the pace. Borrani aluminium rims are now fitted, enclosed 35mm Ceriani forks and telescopic rear shocks. Square slide Dell'Orto carburettors, then new, are fitted. Note the early 750 tank badge.

BELOW Some Amerian Eagle 750s used an American made fibreglass fuel tank. Here's one. This too is a GT with high bars, now with obligatory side reflectors. Exact numbers imported before American Eagle went bankrupt are confusing, but the best guess is about 100. Some were the 750 S model which was called 750 SS. Only in America!

LAVERDA 750 GT

ABOVE Inside an early 750 Laverda engine. Everything is built to last. There are many 100,000-mile engines that have made it without overhaul. (*Cycle World*)

ABOVE LEFT Laverda factory promotional postcard, this time of the 750 GT of 1971/72, with a full range of factory accessories. The mirror is wonderful; it appears to be the same one that was used on the 1974 American specification 750 SFC

LEFT 1969 was a turning point; the 750 GT came first in late 1968, then the S in late 1968, early 1969. This is the real start to a stunning line of sports motorcycles. The emphasis has changed from touring to sports, and for the better. Laverda learnt fast. Open carburettors, looking great (if risky to longevity), single seat option, low bars and two-leading shoe front brake from Laverda worked wonders.

The twin cylinders, just slightly inclined, were in light alloy, as was the head, and were fed by two 29mm Dell'Orto carburettors. The sohc was driven by a duplex chain, while valve diameters were 38mm inlet and 34mm exhaust. The crankcase-cum-sump was extensively ribbed and divided horizontally.

At the left-hand-end of the shaft was a twin contact breaker set for the 12-volt battery ignition. A dynamo was clamped to the front of the crankcase and the starter motor was mounted behind the crankcase.

The right side gear pedal was designed for toe operation; the rocking type belatedly consigned to oblivion. There was a five-speed gearbox. The 18in diameter wheel rims were aluminium alloy and were fitted with a 3.5in front and 4in rear tyres. There was a twin leading shoe front brake and a single leading shoe brake at the rear.

Chromium plating was used extensively with the mudguards and brackets, chainguard, headlamp bracket and exposed rear suspension springs so treated, in addition to the usual parts. The four-gallon tank, recessed for knee grips, boasted a parcel carrier.

The 650 was not imported to England and after a

ABOVE 1970/71 750 SF with Laverda's own second generation drum brakes. This will be the last of the open carburettor, knee pad, slim seat version with the exhaust cross-over close to the cylinder head. For some this model is the finest 750; it's easy to see why they have that opinion. The Craven top box spoils this machine.

LEFT 1973 750 SF front drum brake, the brake that gave its name to the machine; SF equals *super freni*, or S model with Laverda-made *freni* or brake.

decades, it was that the 650 was little more than an imitation of the Honda CB72/77 series. Although the detail work must be credited to Luciano Zen, the impetus came from Massimo who had of course been inspired by Honda's 305cc Hawk. If Massimo had the wit and foresight to copy the shape of the Honda's engine, he should be admired for knowing a good thing when he saw one, rather than being reviled as a plagiarist. After all, Honda themselves rose to racing prominence at the start of the decade thanks in no small measure to their use of four-valve heads, and that was regarded as a stroke of genius. The fact that the Rudge concern had pioneered such heads some thirty years earlier was conveniently forgotten.

Of more enduring significance than the 650, although differing little in detail, was its big brother the 750, released to the world's press in May 1968. The British importers and press, insular as ever, pretty much ignored the bike: others were more far-sighted. The Benelux countries, to become a fruitful source of Laverda sales, enjoyed the benefit of an enthusiastic importer and it was a Dutch journalist, Gerhard Klomps, who first released details of the bike to the UK via the pages of *The Motor Cycle*.

The larger bike was built not particularly in a quest for more power and speed for its own sake, but to offer better acceleration. The tubular frame dispensed with the standard front downtubes and the top tubes were virtually hidden by the tank, all of which inevitably focussed attention on the Honda look-alike engine that was the machine's most imposing feature. Bored out to 80mm, to produce a displacement of 744cc, it was compact and undeniably striking, thanks to its square finning which conferred a modern aspect.

The machine was potent looking and yet attractive, with side panels covering the battery and toolkit, and with an extensive use of shiny chrome. The frame came in any colour so long as it was black, but the purchaser had a choice of white, yellow, red, green or blue for the tank and panels.

On the road, the clutch gained a reputation as being smooth and clean but a little heavy, while the gear-change was rapid and secure, audibly clicking into place. The front brake was described, perhaps just a touch chauvinistically, by *Motociclismo* as 'superlative – there is no fear of finding yourself suddenly brakeless as you do with some foreign bikes!' Admittedly the rear brake was less efficient, with its performance noticeably suffering in the wet.

The machine's weight – some 480 lb – detracted from its acceleration, but nevertheless from a standing start a quarter-mile could be covered in 14.2 seconds thanks to the engine's power (52bhp), while top speed was a more than healthy 110 mph. The unwelcome bulk did offer one boon: straightline stability was excellent even in a fierce side wind. In curves there was a tendency for the bike to take charge and the front wheel

modest hundred or so had been built, the factory was already producing the enlarged edition, the 750; but *Motociclismo* managed to get their sticky paws on a model to report on its virtues or otherwise.

The major criticism was that the pseudo sporty riding position, with the footrests set back, threw too much weight onto the wrists, so that in-town riding soon became tiring. Additionally, the over-wide tank forced the rider's legs unnaturally far apart, which problem was exacerbated at high speed by wind pressure. Fortunately, these defects were offset to some extent by the ample seat which was soft and comfortable and by the unimpeachable suspension, with three settings available at the rear.

Two minor criticisms were levelled at the steed. First, there was a slight but noticeable tremble through the handlebars. Second, although the electric starting was efficient, the *Motociclismo* testers, traditionalists to a man, would have preferred a kick start!

If there was one universal objection to the design, and indeed the grumble has lingered through the

ABOVE 1973 model SF1s are easy to identify because of the use of the CEV (BSA/Triumph-like) headlamp and Lucas (Norton-like) switchgear. The chassis, exhaust system, horns, tank and more lasted the final three years. Gone are the Smiths instruments, replaced by Nippon Denso from Japan. SF1 was used to designate the second series SF.

RIGHT It's 1974 and the SF gets Brembo disc brakes, 280mm discs to be precise with F08 calipers, and new 38mm Ceriani forks. The rear is still the familiar Laverda drum with Ceriani shocks. This machine is an SF2 model but is rare in that it only uses one front disc. Many thought these were SF1 models, two discs meaning SF2. 'SF2' simply meant front disc brakes.

pattering suffered on the prototypes was not entirely eliminated by the time the 750 was in production.

In 1969 the standard models were dubbed 'GT', Gran Turismo, to distinguish them from the newly launched sports version, the 'S' model. The GT did however enjoy some modest refinements. The front brake was waterproofed while the pitiful back brake was ditched in favour of that designed for the S, which was an altogether more powerful affair. Also cribbed from the S were the 30mm carburettors, replacing the 29mm versions on the 1968 bikes. Power was increased to 53bhp at 6,600rpm, with an attendant increase in top speed to approximately 115 mph and a similar improvement in acceleration. The GT also enjoyed a revised tank; it had been slimmed down to offer more comfort for the long-distance rider.

The GT changed little during its production run, but in 1974 it became the GTL. The meaning of the 'L' remains uncertain, although it could be 'Lusso', or 'Luxury'. The GTL was in essence a softer version of the SF, a derivative of the S. It borrowed an SF frame, retained drum brakes and had a detuned engine. The GTL featured a rear hand rail, a less sporting seat than the SF, different side panels and a deeper tank.

It was to be the GT's contemporary, the S, that really stirred the hornet's nest and set the marque on the road to cult status – which it was to attain within a remarkably short time.

The S appeared in 1969, as a logical development of the original 750. The tank was narrowed and shortened and was bereft of its chrome package carrier as befitted a would-be sports machine, although in practice this merely accentuated the baggage problem. The saddle was also modified so that it became virtually a single seat

affair with a raised tail section. The mudguards were tinkered with, but for the rest, the bike repeated the lines and features of the GT.

The S was merely the trail-blazer; it did not last beyond 1970 when it was superseded by the SF – Sport Freni (i.e. brakes). The SF, developed a step behind its track sibling, the SFC, broadly came in four generations that can be rapidly identified as follows:

1. SF: 1970 to late 1972
2. SF1: 1972/73 – drum brakes
3. SF2: 1973/75 – one or two discs at the front
4. SF3: 1975 – cast wheels with triple disc brakes.

A couple of the SF models made their UK debut at the Horticultural Hall Show over that winter, displayed by the recently appointed importers Slater Brothers whose enthusiasm for the factory's products was to play such a major part in bringing the marque to the attention of the British press and potential purchasers. No sooner had the bikes taken their places on their stands than a thief purloined the fuel cap of one, while the other was sold at £695 in kit form to avoid purchase tax. Had the SF been assembled, its price would have been over £800, whereas it was retailing in Italy at the equivalent of £630. For comparison, the new BMW R75/5 was also on offer at the Show, at over £1,100.

By late 1972, the SF1 was available. The engine still endured criticism for being little more than an enlarged Honda; Laverda must have been heartily sick of that particular press chestnut. True, the power plant had hardly been developed from that of the early 750 bikes. However, 36mm carburettors were now employed and the compression ratio had been dropped from the 9.5:1 of the S to 8.9:1, enabling three-star petrol to be used.

New exhaust pipes, uncharacteristically ugly to some eyes, were introduced to comply with strict silencing laws recently introduced in Germany.

The starter motor was mounted behind the engine over the gearbox and the crankshaft was turned via a single row chain. At the right-hand-end of the crankshaft was the dynamo drive pulley with the belt drive running to the forward mounted dynamo. The left-hand-end was also crowded, with a treble sprocket to take the triplex primary drive chain, then a smaller gear running to the oil pump drive gear. Hence, the engine was particularly wide and safety bars were available as an optional extra, although when put to the test they were found to be too flimsy to be useful.

The crankcase split horizontally to reveal its innards and those of the five-speed gearbox. The wet clutch was housed at the left hand of the box and the gearchange

ABOVE The 750 GT never did use disc brakes. This is a 1975 model partly to police specification; screen (although not usually this type), single seat, panniers (for radio equipment) and radio pad behind the seat. Some used an alternator in place of the dynamo, this one didn't. Note polished fork yokes, fork gaiters and big headlamp. A good police bike.

ABOVE RIGHT American specification SF2 with high bars and 1000 tail lamp. No side reflectors but left side gearchange! Not much had happened in the US market after the American Eagle fiasco until 1974. Unfortunately things didn't improve much with a series of importers.

pedal was on the right, although a kit of shafts and cables was made available so that the latter could be swapped to the left to enable the bike to sell in the USA.

The dynamo and starter motor were Bosch components. From Fiamm came the twin horns, generally regarded with satisfaction, for a magnificent roar bellowed forth instead of the usual wet bleat. The electrical controls were by Lucas with the dipswitch, horn and cut-out button on the left and the indicators and starter on the right. The Smiths tachometer and speedometer were soon adjudged not up to the required standards and were ditched in favour of Nippon Denso products.

The frame retained its singular configuration with the engine still forming part of the chassis. There were two bulky top tubes running from the steering head to the rear of the dual seat. Another two tubes looped up

from the rear swinging arm pivot, joining the top tubes for approximately 12 inches, and then curving down to the bottom of the steering head. The general consensus was that the frame worked and the high-speed weave evident on earlier models had been eliminated in the SF1. Slaters had attrributed some, if not all, of the wobble to the Metzeler tyres and they were scrapped in favour of Pirellis. Front and rear suspension units were still of Ceriani manufacture while the Laverda brake, of 230mm, remained outstanding.

Testing the machine, that August the heavyweight journal *Motorcycle Sport* opined that 'this has to be one of the best motorcycles made.' It then, in its own words, 'put the boot in' by stating, somewhat uncharitably, that 'making every allowance for our own prejudices, one was still forced to the conclusion that, when the chips are down, it has this built-in problem. It is still a

The GTL test bike at rest.

vertical twin. Naturally, this has virtues as well, but it has one big, almost unsurmountable, vice: a vertical twin by its very definition vibrates and even Laverda, with what must rate as one of the most robust, carefully designed and assembled engines made, have been unable completely to cure the problem.'

The other side of the coin was that the vertical twin engine had an abundance of power. It had a snappiness available to few other cylinder layouts, a 'gutsiness'. The 65 horses at 7,000rpm had to propel what was a heavy machine at about 480 lb, but took it quite happily to 120 mph.

One noticeable downside was the extravagant fuel consumption. The SF had returned a consistent 50mpg whereas the larger carburettors, lower compression ratio and redesigned camshaft meant that the SF1's performance hovered between 40 and 45mpg – which was not offset by the reduced costs offered by three-star petrol.

Laverda's next offering, the SF2, was available from 1973 to 1975. The overall impression of the machine is that it was a modest variation on a theme that was now five years old and was in danger of becoming outdated. *Motor Cycle News* tested a Slater-prepared model in April 1974, put it through a speed trap at 110 mph and noted caustically that the same speed had been available from 650s fifteen years earlier.

The most significant change was the introduction of single or dual disc braking at the front. *MCN*'s test machine was fitted with a 280mm hydraulically operated twin-disc version that was applauded as superb with a truly progressive and powerful action – sufficient to make the tyre squeal in the dry without causing any anxious moments in the wet. By contrast, the rear twin leading shoe brake required heavy pressure and was really quite disappointing.

At the end of *MCN*'s two-week 700-mile test, part of the rear carrier had been lost thanks to the vibration, the indicators had failed and the pilot bulb had blown. The tester concluded that he liked the SF2 as a machine to ride but then he had not bought it – at £1,250.

The final outpouring of the SF theme was the SF3, still sporting twin Brembo discs at the front but now with a single at the rear, with cast wheels; otherwise to all intents and purposes a re-born SF2. Road test quibbles over the SF3 were that the riding position, with the handlebars too far forward, was uncomfortable for the smaller rider; and the machine's vibration remained excessive. The major criticism levelled at the bike concerned its gearbox that had a disconcerting propensity to find false neutrals while the real neutral was difficult to find unless it was snicked in before coming to a stop.

Such is the similarity of the SF3 to the earlier SFs that all these criticisms might have been applied to them too. Or had the road-tester forgotten?

Nevertheless, the SF3 had many fine qualities. For performance, *Motorcycle Sport* adjudged it to be on a par with a Norton Commando, faster than a BMW 800 and only a shade slower than a Suzuki GS750. But its real *forte* was its handling, described by *MCS* as 'quite a revelation, impeccable.' In an extensive series of tests on the best production motorcycles, *MCS* designated the Suzuki GS1000 as inexplicably twitchy, the Gold Wing as heavy and rather vague, but the SF3 as convincingly in a class of its own in the handling stakes.

By the latest standards, the SF3 was undoubtedly outdated in many respects but it oozed 'character'. In the words of *Motorcycle Sport*, the SF3 was the last flowering of 'a high class hooligan of the '60s . . . aimed at the dedicated without pretence of being the smoothest, fastest or most comfortable.'

GTL 750: Phil Todd

Often dismissed as a bit of an oddity, the 750 GTL was a purpose-built touring machine, substantially different to its 750 SF stablemate. The Italian Post Office and many police forces were equipped with the GTL.

The flip-up seat is far more plush and comfortable than the SF. It blends in with the rear of the rounded fuel tank to give a good riding position; it also soaks up nearly all the vibes that 360-degree twins tend to put out.

The motor has the ultra heavy crankshaft from the earlier GT model. The valves, cams and carbs are the same 'soft' performance items too. This all makes for a much reduced level of vibration all round, and a motor that feels like it would tow a caravan up a cliff!

I know a parallel twin is not the best format for a tourer these days, but the GTL is one of the best, even by today's standards. Its ability to pull top gear from about half an rpm, the fabulous handling, modern type switchgear and the large (properly rubber mounted) Bosch headlamp still make this machine a serious contender for anyone considering a touring bike that is a little bit different.

The GTL is one of my favourite Laverdas. If you ever have the chance to ride one, you will know why. Price-wise they are usually cheaper than an SF but, with about the same rarity as a 750 SFC, the GTL must eventually soar in value.

Phil Todd testing the GTL.

America and the 750 twin

Undeniably, Massimo Laverda had his eye on the American market in 1965 with his concept of the big twin. Triumph, BSA and Norton, and to some extent Harley-Davidson, were ruling the fast sportsbike market. Honda were undoubtedly in control of volume sales, albeit with smaller capacity machinery. Massimo's plan of attack was therefore to build a Triumph that looked like a Honda with BMW quality. Surely, that was a reasonable approach. But there was a fatal flaw: how could Laverdas be production engineered and then be sold like Hondas?

Jack McCormack, ex-Triumph on the road sales rep, ex-Suzuki US marketing, formed American Eagle with several more experienced partners as a year-round outdoor activity vehicle sales organisation; motorcycles and off-road buggies in the summer, snowmobiles in the winter. Sales, not manufacturing, note.

Kawasaki, Sprite and Laverda supplied the motorcycles all under the symbol of the bald eagle. The whole operation was an unmitigated disaster lasting no more than a couple of years of real trading. Everyone lost money.

Laverda supplied some 150 Trail motorcycles as well as some 750 twins in GT and S form. Each kind of motorcycle came either with factory tanks and seats or American-made fibreglass. Just how many entered the US is unknown, but it can only be a few handfuls. The greatest misfortune is that this false start soured the name of Laverda in the US for some time to come and left a bad taste for the decision makers in Breganze. Massimo never fulfilled his prime ambition with the 750 in the 'world's largest marketplace'.

The first 750 twins sold in the USA were sold under the American Eagle label. Here's a GT from 1969. There were a number of specification changes in the batches that were imported. Apart from the high bars, the major change was the tank badge. Only the marketing was a disaster; the motorcycles – essentially the same as those succeeding in Europe – were misunderstood. (*Cycle World*)

SF2 versus SF3: Tim Parker

25,000 miles of street riding shared between a 1974 SF2 and a 1975 SF3 back in the mid-1970s taught me a lot. The main things were that reliability counts for more than speed and that later does not mean better.

In the early summer of 1975 I went on the *Motorcyclist Illustrated* Monte Carlo Rally organised in conjunction with BMW. Effectively, this meant a flat-out blast through France on a combination of autoroute and the Route Napoleon. Somehow I tagged onto two experienced riders both on then-new R90S BMWs; my SF2 was just an SF2. Nice, but nothing special. On the autoroute I could hold only about 90 mph for any length of time; rider weakness, not the bike. Next day in the mountains I never saw anyone else except when my Laverda cut out periodically. The engine would stop and then would start again. Finally, after about the fifth time I decided to find out what it was. I could not stand the BMWs passing.

An ignition wire in the harness close to the steering-head was cracked, because it was too tight. Once fixed, the machine was magnificent. I felt that the SF2 would nurture and coerce a middling rider into becoming a competent, fast rider. Once on the move it was not too heavy, nor the clutch too stiff, the riding position too 'long'. It possessed a rhythm, a balance that few motorcycles do. That character, perhaps that alone, the Triple never had. As for speed and handling it would match any contemporary Ducati, BMW, Guzzi or Norton once on the road.

My SF3 which I owned in 1977 should have been the same to ride, but was not. Other experienced SF3 owners have said the same. What makes the difference is hard to fathom because mechanically, except for the new cast wheels, all is the same. Maybe the stiffness and thus 'harshness' of the wheels does not suit the chassis? Maybe the rhythm of the engine does not either. Or maybe it was my particular machine?

As my SF2 was a paragon of virtue, so my SF3 was always in trouble. The last straw was a mighty explosion on the M1, of all places, at something over 100 mph. A circlip came out to cause valve destruction, or maybe the other way around. I have the bent rod still attached to the horrible piston today.

But like all Laverdas, another inherent quality, it was easy to repair. I sold it in perfect shape to make way for a 750 SFC. The 750 twins take some riding under your tank bag to get to know. To a machine, they are always rewarding.

The Twins – A Retrospective: Tim Isles

There is perhaps not a great deal that qualifies me to write this piece about the twins other than that I have owned Laverdas for many years. I would not pretend to be either a particularly skilled mechanic or a hard rider,

but the bikes have given me a lot of pleasure over the years.

Like many, it was those rorty Jotas that were my introduction to the marque. The arrival of the triple in 1973 coincided with the production of the 14,000th twin, a machine that had been Moto Laverda's mainstay since its introduction in 1968. Production of the 750 in tourer, sportster and racer form was to continue until 1976, by which time a further 5,000 or so units had been produced.

It is a fact that with the introduction of the 1,000 triple, its smaller brother was from then on destined

always to be in its shadow. Besides, the 750 class, by the mid-1970s, was seen as a leftover from a previous era as all manufacturers worth their salt had a 1-litre bike as their flagship.

But it is worth remembering one fact. When a horde of journalists used to descend on Breganze to hurl the firm's resonating triple into the nearby mountains, prior to waxing lyrical with tales of stupendous performance, they were nearly always tracked unerringly by a factory mechanic, or even Massimo's brother Piero, on a tired-looking orange hack. That it could boast only two cylinders and a quarter-litre less capacity seemed

1974 SF2 shortly after collection from Collington, Slater Brothers' premises. Still on original Pirelli tyres, it features two factory accessories, the rear carrier and safety bars. The colour was factory original, metallic black. Note the Fiamm horns and the large exhaust cross-over pipe under the engine. Co-author Tim Parker's first Laverda; a superb motorcycle.

to escape our scribes' notice; but perhaps it would have been unfair to mention the point, lest it tarnish the glitter of the new machine.

The 750 never enjoyed great sales in the UK. A ready-made market in continental Europe took care of as many as could be produced and when efforts were made to market the machine in the UK it was largely regarded as neither fish nor fowl by the public. And who could blame them? They would not know that factory-prepared examples had obliterated the opposition in endurance races and the only products from Breganze that Joe Public might have come across were a rather feeble scooter, the moped, or perhaps the slightly quaint 200cc twin. Hence the svelte, sophisticated SF of 1971/72 did not receive the hearty welcome it deserved.

Market forces would not permit the 750 twin to attain the fame of its bigger brother, despite journalists like L.J.K. Setright and David Minton singing its praises: such accolades largely fell on deaf ears. True, its price was considerably more than that of a Norton Commando, but this could be totally justified by a standard of engineering that was years ahead of its British equivalent.

Strangely, or perhaps inevitably, the rise of the classic movement has generated renewed interest in these roadsters. Always rare in the UK, demand now has to be satisfied by importing used examples from the Continent. The few dealers report business as very brisk in the parts line and good examples of the models can fetch fancy prices. A band of gladiators campaign their machines in the UK with considerable success in the classic racing circus and interest generally is high.

So what is the attraction of the roadsters? Probably not their looks. For beauty, which only the Italians can achieve so totally, you had to turn to its rare and exquisite cousin the SFC of which but 500 or so were made. Although sharing all the virtues of their road-going relations, the SFCs, as special framed competition shop racers, cannot in all fairness be included in the equation. No, you have to live with the roadsters to appreciate their virtues.

The 750s were, and in good condition still are, very handy high-speed tourers. A good, and I stress 'good', example is a delight to ride. Vibration, usually a problem in any large parallel twin, is there but within bounds, while the handling is vice free and totally predictable. For proof, go and watch the racers at play, for these machines handle with the best.

The ride is too firm for most people's taste. The original rear Ceriani shock absorbers are harsher than necessary and the Ceriani front forks of the later SF2s and SF3s are not delicate instruments either. Softening both fore and aft does not affect stability in any way, but of course in these days when originality is sacrosanct, you should keep hold of your factory parts.

Brakes? There are no substitutes for the Brembo

discs fitted to the SF2 and SF3 models. If you own an SF2 with one disc on the front you just might find it marginal, but most had a pair and, of course, the SF3 had a disc on the rear as well. You should not, however, let this put you off the earlier models with their identical 2 l.s. 230mm units back and front. To work efficiently, they must be set up correctly but then should not be found wanting in road use, unless you are towing a caravan or ride very hard indeed. Admittedly, the front drum cannot really cope with the demands of the race track and the factory recognised this by offering the 4 l.s. Ceriani as an option on their production-drum-braked SFCs.

The performance of a standard machine is more than respectable and if your engine is in good order there is no reason why it should not be used to the full. Top speed, a fairly academic subject, is a shade under 120 mph for the S and SF models, and perhaps 110 mph for the GT and GTL versions. More important, the machine will sit for hour after hour with 6,000rpm showing on the tacho and 100 mph on the speedo.

A boost in power came with the big valve head and 36mm carbs first seen on the 1973 SF1, but the increased weight of the model, plus a need to civilise across the range to meet stricter legislation, bringing with it lower compression ratios and heftier silencers, negated any increase in performance that might have been expected from the other modifications.

Mechanically, the machines are easy to work on but as with any high-performance machinery you cannot take short cuts. A rebuild should be just that, and there is no point in putting worn parts back into an engine that has been lovingly taken apart. A healthy engine will give many thousands of miles. A botched job will at best be a disappointment in terms of vibration and performance levels; at worst it will destroy itself.

At the time of writing, availability of parts is generally good in the UK, but they can be expensive. Without wishing to be vilified by the small number of dealers in the UK, it is worth mentioning that many parts – such as bearings, chains, batteries, fork seals etc – are proprietary items and can be obtained from your local dealer at a substantial saving. Check out prices with the local Guzzi or Ducati man where they stock the same equipment. Before the 750s became popular many were broken up, so if it is cycle parts you are short of, then peruse the 'for sale' columns or place an advert. The bits are around.

Which one to buy? They are all good, although if performance is a major factor in your choice then perhaps a GT or GTL is not for you. For pure looks you might choose the rare 750 S but be sure you get a real one whch had Grimeca brakes. A very few of the first SFs carried the lovely tank of the S; but if it has Laverda brakes then it ain't an S.

The SF2 gives classic appeal wire wheels and a disc or two on the front to slow you down, but the 38mm

It's unclear just how many SF3s were made; whatever the number, it can only have been a few. Officially a 1976 model, many remained unsold through 1977. This is co-author Tim Parker's machine which is stock except for BMW indicators, motocross fork gaiters and reversed fork legs – all as experiments, all prove not very much. Nice, but not as nice as the SF2. Cast wheels didn't suit the chassis as they did the 1000. (Tim Parker)

forks made for a heftier look to the machine which is not dispelled when you take it for a canter over twisty roads. The most practical is probably the SF3; but for me, those alloy wheels and the fibreglass seat tail piece do not make for an integrated whole, especially when compared with its forbears.

For what it's worth, my favourite is the SF1 of 1973, a machine born out of the drum-braked SFC. Whichever you choose, consider the following guidelines. First, buy one with matching frame and engine numbers, and second, be wary of a machine that deviates greatly from standard. I mention these two points because original examples command far higher resale values. Third, if you can afford it, spend a little more to buy a good bike. As I write, £1,500 buys a scruffy one, £2,000 a nice one and £2,750 the best. Do your sums well when considering a tatty one. Some, to quote Laverda expert Phil Todd, can bite you as you walk past them. If you go for a rebuild project, arm yourself with a good set of tools and Tim Parker's Green Book. They are simple machines to work on and eminently pleasing to restore.

To conclude, I think it is true to say that it is only now that the virtues of the 750 roadster are being fully recognised. Indeed, many a triple owner has an SF to complement it. Possibly the twins lacked the charisma of the triples but I will say that you have to look very hard indeed to find a motorcycle from the 1970s that does so many things so well. Sportster, tourer, ride-to-work commuter: it can manage them all.

SFC

In recent years the SFC – SF Competizione – has attained legendary status as the undisputed flagship of the Laverda marque. Of the 19,000 or so 750cc twins produced, a mere 549 were SFC versions. They were in reality thoroughbred endurance racers available to the privateer but they could be thinly disguised for exceptionally high speed road use.

In 1969 and 1970 the factory had campaigned on the European continental endurance circuit with specially prepared 750 S and SF models. Although they met with some success they were never more than handily fettled sports bikes. Massimo and his colleague Zen appreciated that to compete at the top level a purpose-built racer was the order of the day. The SFC duly appeared in 1971, and was instantly successful, taking the laurels at Montjuich Park in the Barcelona 24 Hours.

The first-generation drum-brake SFC was, to a degree, a development of the early SF – hence the name. Again, as the name denotes, it was intended principally for competition use and it duly sported a simple racing seat, a half fairing and rear-mounted footrests.

It was also finished off in the bright orange paintwork attributed to the factory's race hardware. The vivid, even lurid, orange colouring had been chosen so that the factory race mechanics could readily identify their machines at night in the blaze of the lights illuminating the pit straight during a 24-hour marathon – and not simply because the Laverda agricultural division had a surplus of combine paint (actually red) as some uncharitable wags would have it!

Be that as it may, a large proportion of the SFCs actually took to the roads, as the factory would fix a horn and incorporate a number plate in the tail. Perhaps a latter-day comparison could be made with the Formula One world championship-winning RC30 that in the late 1980s was the ultimate development of Honda's already successful vee-four 750cc range; a racer in road-bike guise, a wolf in sheep's clothing.

Although there was more than a passing resemblance to the road-going twins, the SFC was vitally different, engine and chassis, from stem to stern; very few parts were interchangeable with the GT, S and SF models.

At the heart of the beast was still the familiar sohc vertical twin at 80 × 74mm, a 360-degree design with horizontally split crankcase, wet sump and an integral five-speed box. The camshaft drive, running between the cylinders, was by duplex chain while the primary drive was by triplex.

The two valves were set at 70 degrees, with the inlet valve at $32\frac{1}{2}$ degrees to the cylinder axis and the exhaust valve at $37\frac{1}{2}$ degrees. Initially, the inlet valve was 38mm and the exhaust 34mm.

In standard trim the early SFCs used special pistons giving a compression ratio of 9.8:1, as well as Spanish-made Amal 36mm carburettors. Every item of the engine was selected by the race shop and heat-treated to ensure maximum reliability. Special features abounded inside the SFC engine. For instance, the main and big end roller bearings were to endurance racing specification and a larger capacity oil pump ensured that they never ran dry. In addition, a close-ratio gearbox was fitted.

The motors were finally assembled to racing tolerances and prepared to produce 70bhp at 7,500rpm, sufficient to take the steed to 125 mph. The battery was still charged by a car-type Bosch dynamo, weighing 11 lb, driven by a rubber vee belt.

The frame, similar to, but not the same as, that of the SF, was a huge open affair with a spine consisting of four 40mm tubes from which was slung the engine. The tubes were attached to the cambox at four points and to frame plates which mated with the rear of the crankcase. The tubular swinging arm featured a cross brace just to the rear of the pivot.

Although the frame employed the same geometry as the roadgoing SF, visually it was very different, with bosses for the fairing and rear set footrests. The bracketry under the seat was greatly modified to take a different battery tray and electrics, and the twin coils were mounted on the top rails under the side panels to allow rapid access. There was no lifting handle to be found to ease the machine onto its special narrow centre stand, nor was there a prop stand.

From the first, 35mm Ceriani forks were fitted at the front, with the same manufacturer's units fitted at the rear. The brakes were Laverda's own 230mm drums initially, although the very special works racers featured a double-sided Ceriani, as the factory units were overtaxed on the race tracks. (Triple discs appeared in 1974; there was never a mixture as on the SF2.)

The factory produced 85, 79 and 3 drum-brake SFCs in 1971, 1972 and 1973 respectively. The lowly number in 1973 is explained by the company's preoccupation

TOP This is a very early 750 SFC; it's a 1971/72 model, (actually painted the familiar orange but because the photograph was over-exposed the photo-printer had to compensate too much). Note extended headlamp, Amal carburettors, notched tank and 'straight' exhaust. It appears to have the special Ceriani racing drum brakes. Handsome, isn't it?

ABOVE This machine was for sale at the Imola moto jumble in the mid 1980s. Another 1973 model with the underslung, cross-over exhaust, still with two silencers. Not a bad buy! Tank decal isn't stock nor is the caption 'World Champions'. (Tim Parker)

with the move to new premises on the edge of Breganze.

A particular feature of the 1971 models was the protruding headlamp, that jars to most eyes; it was flush on subsequent versions. There was, however, little consistency in detail on these so-called production racers (although the term does not really describe their nature). They were built in batches with whatever came to hand in the race shop and were constantly being updated.

Inconsistency characterises the whole production run, and frames differed in minutiae. Similarly, a number of different exhaust systems were used. Very early machines employed short down pipes and enormously long megaphones. By late 1971, longer down pipes and shorter megaphones were in favour, albeit still running beside rather than under the engine. For 1972, the system featured crossover tubes under the sump, and the option of silencers was available. Very early SFCs were fitted with alloy petrol tanks of 25-litre capacity but by late 1971 these had been changed to fibreglass.

Anarchy ruled in later years, as privateers added steering dampers, replaced the original fibreglass with alloy tanks and generally modified their bikes as racers will, in the generally misguided belief that they know better than the factory.

In 1974, what amounted to the second generation SFC made its debut; and it was visually quite different. Apart from the obvious discs, by Brembo, and magnesium rear wheel hub, it boasted bigger 38mm Ceriani forks, a slimmer and lower tank, a revised half fairing and side panels partially shrouding a lower and longer frame, which had been introduced to lower the centre of gravity and hence improve handling. For road use, a pair of silencers, similar to those of the late drum-brake models, was available, whereas for the race track the twin exhausts were scrapped in favour of a two-into-one reverse cone exiting on the left-hand-side.

LEFT **1972/73 Laverda drum-brake 750 SFC in the studio. Fork legs were painted orange but the centre stand was black. Note the early 'solid' gear lever and Dunlop 4.10 TT100 tyres. No one is sure if the rear seat competition number roundel was production or just for the photograph.**

ABOVE **Late 1973 model SFC with the late type silencers subsequently used through 1976. This is a factory promotional postcard. Weight is quoted as 210 kilogrammes. The headlamp is now flush. Original SFCs have the letters 'SFC' under the lower left engine lug.**

A new, lighter crankshaft was fitted to these later SFCs and the engine was tweaked with a variation in valve sizes, to 41.5mm for the inlet and 35.5mm for the exhaust. The plug angles were also revised, while a new cam was adopted and the pistons were changed, with the compression ratio upped to 10.5:1. A pair of 36mm Dell'Orto carburettors, without pump jets, was employed henceforth. Accordingly, power was upped to 75 bhp at 7,500rpm and top speed to 130 mph.

222 of these 'disc/points' SFCs were built in 1974 and a batch (probably of 50 but some would say as many as 100) found their way to the USA. They featured Jota instruments and bars instead of the standard clip-ons, a 3C rectangular, instead of a round, CEV tail lamp and, those rare birds, indicators; together with the refinements of a mirror and side reflectors.

For the following year, developments continued apace. A major change was that the twin contact breaker points were dropped in favour of an electronic ignition

trigger, to be found under a small housing in a new magnesium primary chaincase cover replacing the previous light alloy affair. There were significant changes to the cylinder head, necessitating revised barrels and pistons, that were not readily interchangeable with those off the 1974 bikes. An oil cooler was now a standard fitting. These machines came to be known as 'Electronica' versions and 130 were made. They were the fastest of all SFCs.

Late 1975 saw the final edition that was fitted with Laverda's own thin-web cast alloy wheels, as an option. A modest 30 were built, mostly in 1976.

For the last two years of its life, in Elecronica form, a special cam was available as an optional extra, raising the rpm at which peak power was made. Speed was never quoted by the factory for the Electronica but an Italian magazine put one through the traps at 138 mph.

Like all the SFCs, there was a simple CEV combined lights/starter/horn switch fitted. A popular modifi-

LEFT Modified 1974
SFC photographed in
Breganze in 1989.
(Raymond Ainscoe)

BELOW LEFT Factory
shot of the standard
1975 model.

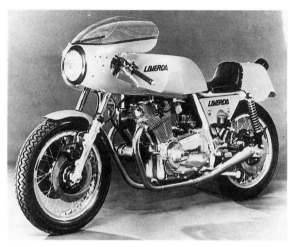

ABOVE LEFT Rare 1976 model fitted with factory cast
wheels. White tank and side panel decals are unusual.
Apart from the handlebar mirror and black rear
springs this machine looks stock. The Nippon Denso
instruments were likely fitted in England by the Slater
Brothers. (Tim Parker)

LEFT Early 1974-spec SFC. It's not quite finished
because it lacks a horn (even the little tab to mount
one) and decals. Note the Brembo discs, the front
wheel from the 3C/SF2, and the rear hub in
magnesium and disc unique to the model. The centre
stand is now silver. Look closely, this one has a
crankcase breather where the dip stick would usually be.

cation was to fit twin Lucas coils to replace the original
Nippon Denso coil in an effort to ease starting. Initially
all SFCs used a Smiths rev counter on a bracket to the
left of the headlamp. However, a few of the tiny number
of SFCs that found their way into the UK were
converted to Nippon Denso rev counters and speedos,
similar to those sent to the USA.

Perversely, Slaters imported no more than half a
dozen or so of these orange beasties but with the passage
of almost twenty years the model has attained almost
cult status. Hand in hand with 'classic' standing has
come a startling escalation in prices over the late 1980s
and a small but steady flow of imports has seen the
numbers in the UK rise to about 25.

Would-be purchasers should note that original machines sport the letters 'SFC' under the lower left
engine lug. Although the frames were not specially
numbered, being mixed in willy-nilly with the standard
twin cylinder range, their numbers were prefixed with
either 750 C, in the case of the drum brake models, or
750 C2 for the disc versions, while engine and frame
numbers were the same.

Unlike some exotica, the SFC is so different from its
roadster cousin that it is a very difficult machine to
replicate. A thriving SFC register exists, contactable via
the International Laverda Owners Club, with full
details of correct frame and engine numbers, ready to
assist any would-be purchasers. Nevertheless, in these
days of escalating prices, as always, the maxim remains:
caveat emptor!

Riding a 750 SFC – street and track:
Tim Parker

Most people have never ridden the bike of their choice prior to purchase. Dealers and private individuals are still pretty reluctant to let you try their offerings. It was the same when I first obtained my SFC. Obviously, I was mesmerised by the bike's looks and its history. My first SFC was frankly a wreck. Complete, but sorry. I hauled it home in pieces and then spent about nine months assembling it all. I never looked inside the engine; I just put it all together and proceeded to ride it, home-tuned so to speak, for about a year on the street. It was both horrible and exhilarating. Horrible because the engine was tired which meant it wouldn't idle and didn't want to start and when revved vibrated beyond holding. Exhilarating because it was remarkably comfortable, very stable if stiffly sprung and, in spite of its tiredness, was indeed very responsive. I rode several times with a good friend on a faithful, well-tuned Mark 1 Moto Guzzi Le Mans – the SFC was an easy match. And this was in 1983, when few cared about these machines. I remember one occasion when after 200 miles of rain we reached the M1 north to Donington in the dry. In an attempt to dry ourselves out we held 115 mph or thereabout for around 20 miles. It was heaven sent.

In town the SFC was hell. With the world's stiffest clutch pull, no idle, reluctant re-starting and the reach across the tank there's no other description. And to make matters worse, pot holes and no time to enjoy the gorgeous exhaust note. With either dual silencers or the two-into-one megaphone the bike was equally noisy but it wasn't that harsh, nasty loudness; more an exciting note that gives pleasure to most anyone, much to their surprise. Two years after that I decided to race the bike, first with a stock but freshened engine and then more seriously with a considerably modified cylinderhead. Eventually all the unnecessary street equipment was stored, as was the original bodywork to be replaced with replica everything: although nothing was altered in such a way that it couldn't be restored perfectly. At that final stage my SFC, at least, had truly blossomed.

It starts, idles and carburates perfectly through to 9400rpm with little vibration and no hesitation. And it has done so reliably for a long time. On the dynomometer I use it peaks at 91 horsepower at the crankshaft – several stock SFCs have recorded between 65 and 67 horsepower on the same dyno. It runs on air filters too. It's competitive with the Ducati 750 SS and XR-750 Harley-Davidson, is faster than any Norton Commando and is close behind most Rob North Tridents. Its handling and braking is on a par with any of the best with considerably softened but stock suspension. Frankly, the only major modification is to the rear

wheel; the original disc brake rear hubs were magnesium and it's considered too risky to race with them, now that even the youngest is fifteen or more years old. A contemporary GS750 Suzuki rear hub is laced to a DID rim; more weight but more strength.

The 750 SFC makes an excellent road racing bike.

Not a sprinter, you understand, but a darn good middle distance or endurance bike. Exactly as when it was new it carries only one disadvantage in comparison with its peers – weight. You never feel it at the controls once rolling, but of course it's always there. For some of us, its looks and its noise win every time.

Co-author Tim Parker aboard his 1975 750 SFC electronica – see the altered primary drive cover – during a Classic Racing Motorcycle Club between-the-races parade in 1984. Note the oil cooler radiator and the factory two-into-one exhaust. (Peter Wileman)

Triples: 3C and Jota

1973 marked a significant milestone in Laverda history. Formerly the factory had been located in antiquated premises in the centre of Breganze, turning out a limited number of motorcycles each year, most of which were spoken for. With the encouraging success of the 750cc endurance racers on the tracks, Francesco judged that there was a market available to justify increased production. Accordingly, a rumoured £1,000,000 (but probably more) was invested in a brand-new factory covering 12,000 square metres on the southern edge of town. Francesco's vision was to double output thanks to the introduction of the latest machinery without employing more than the existing 300 staff. But, equally importantly, his hopes were pinned on a new flagship: the 1,000cc triple that had undergone a lengthy gestation period.

A one-litre prototype had been displayed at the Milan Show as long ago as 1969. It was not a serious effort but very much of a three-cylinder-twin bitsa, a one-off assembled from spare parts merely to hint at the shape of things to come. The bore and stroke of the three cylinders measured 75mm and 74mm respectively – the same as the 650 twin, with which it shared an sohc assembly – to produce a capacity of 980.76cc. Its internals were largely borrowed from the GT model. In the words of Piero Laverda: 'It was very smooth with a lot of low-speed power. It sounded beautiful but it was too heavy and too slow. We wanted a sports bike, not a luxury tourer.'

With this aim in mind, an experimental bike appeared in 1970 featuring a full loop frame and twin cams. For a couple of years Luciano Zen toyed with this triple and its progeny, at least one of which reverted to sohc running. But with both the trade and the press baying for action and pressuring the company, the unimaginatively named 3C – 3 cilindri – was launched in 1973. In retrospect, that was at least twelve months too early.

The 3C's engine – the backbone of the marque's quality offerings for the best part of two decades henceforth – was a transverse four-stroke that retained the dimensions of the 1969 prototype. The head was in light alloy and the compression ratio was 9:1. The valves were operated by two camshafts driven by a single chain running between cylinders two and three.

Carburation was via three 32mm Dell'Orto units. Primary drive was by chain, with a five-speed gearbox

in use. Laverda's possibly extravagant claim was that 80bhp was available at 7,250rpm, sufficient to propel the triple to 137 mph. Other touches were the Bosch electronic ignition system, a 12-volt battery and twin horns of outstanding efficiency.

The brakes, in keeping with tradition, were universally regarded as superb. The front double drum, used on the prototype machines and initial production batch of perhaps 50 machines, was soon replaced by double discs, although a drum was retained at the rear.

The double-jointed clip-on bars, subsequently to be called 'Jota bars', enjoyed a wide range of adjustment. The three exhaust pipes flowed to a single junction pipe which in turn divided into two large upswept silencers one on either side.

The new triple came with built-in charisma merely by virtue of being Europe's biggest capacity bike and although the price – £1,400 in the UK – was steep, it was not too daunting to put off the marketing target, the so-called 'discerning enthusiast'. It had a distinctive, hunched-up stance, as though it were ready to leap.

The energetic UK concessionaires, Slater Brothers, claimed in their advertising programme: 'We have the utmost faith in our machines. We do not claim perfection – but what we do claim, and that emphatically, is the quality of ownership designed into every bike … You see where we are aiming. Not at the gimmicky attractions of chrome plating, ancillary lighting, styling and bright colours (although we can beat the opposition on their own ground in this area if so required) but at the basics of fine motorcycling – reliability, safety, longevity and a performance quality above and beyond that of sheer speed (although if required we will beat the opposition there as well).'

What was the reality behind these confident assertions? The heart of the machine, the mighty triple, offered bags of power; in fact possibly too much, as top speed was almost twice Britain's legal maximum. When reading reports of the 3C and its direct descendants, there is one constant plaintive moan: the engine will inevitably propel its rider into the local constabulary's notebook and hence to a magistrate's court!

Fortunately, the cycle parts were capable of harnessing the motor's horses. The full double-cradle frame was conventional, relying on a large-diameter single top tube that was braced horizontally to the steering head and diagonally down to near the swinging-arm pivot.

LEFT The date is 1969. The first Laverda 1000 triple prototype is still recognisable as a 650 twin with a third cylinder; still single overhead cam and everything else much like its smaller brother. Honda's benchmark 750 KO four cylinder had yet to be launched but Laverda decided two cams were necessary for their flagship.

BELOW Luciano Zen aboard another prototype triple, this time with two camshafts and a mixture of cycle parts which did actually reach production. The exact date is uncertain but it's probably late 1972.

1973 production line 3C being used as a factory test machine. Note the additional instrument mounted above the handlebars which are still one-piece. The seat and exhaust pipe have suffered hard work. Big headlamp, wire spoke wheels and drum brakes make this a rare machine today. (Dave Minton)

If the handling was not quite up to what British scribes would describe as unapproachable – a Norton – it was not far off, inspiring confidence, consuming both fast and slow curves with equal facility and forgiving the over-ambitious rider almost any mistakes. Similarly, the suspension was well up to scratch, with Ceriani units front and rear. The large Bosch headlamp came in for high praise, as did the powerful stop light and indicators, while the quality switches were well placed on the bars. Another plus was the comprehensive toolkit.

Summing up these manifold qualities, *Motorcycle Sport* concluded after a test ride: 'It was almost impossible to offer a valid criticism. The standard of workmanship was outstanding . . .'

Sadly, the reality was that there were important defects, at least one of which had a seriously adverse effect on sales in the UK. The Achilles heel was the newly devised transitorised ignition system from Bosch, which belied the manufacturer's reputation as a purveyor of quality electrics. The unreliability and lumpy running was eventually traced by the Bosch technicians to the black box housing connections underneath the petrol tank. Inadequate sealing was permitting water to penetrate and cause a short circuit. By the time the problem was resolved, much damage had been inflicted on both the sales and the reputation of the 3C.

The 3C was also justifiably criticised on other counts. Its weight, some 550 lb with a full tank, did not make for a comfortable ride through town. The dropped handlebars, that no doubt contributed to the sports image that Piero Laverda had hankered after, undoubtedly exacerbated the problem as considerable pressure could build up in the rider's forearms. Another constant source of complaint was the clutch pull, that had first manifested itself on the 750. 'Two hands are really necessary' was the tester's inevitable wail.

When the bike first appeared, the unanimous verdict was that it cried out for shaft drive. This suggestion, born of aesthetics and theory alike, was seemingly justified. For instance, the owner's handbook recommended lubricating the chain every 1,250 miles. However, an *MCS* test machine lasted a paltry 600 miles before the chain had thrown off its lubricant and required adjustment. (As an aside, once slack set in, the chain would contentedly grate the chrome of the offside silencer.)

Another press whinge, although disputed by many riders, was that the gearbox action was both slow and noisy, with a noticeable lull before the transmission

1975 1000 3C with optional single seat. Here's the first
showing of an oil cooler (with horns mounted on it!),
the Jota bars and front disc brakes. With this model
Laverda virtually killed their 750 twin sales overnight.
This machine was big, fast and strong.
(Hans Blomqvist)

accepted the drive after an upward change. A final sour
note concerned the range, quoted by the handbook at
160 miles for the 4½-gallon tank. Although 75mpg were
available at town speeds, the figure dropped to 30mpg
when the bike was on full song, or indeed as low as
8mpg in road racing.

By May 1974, the triple's UK price was up to £1,600
as against £1,250 for the SF2. A month later, the faulty
ignition was recitified and by the autumn a new batch of
3Cs was available with detail modifications to the
exhaust system, a smaller Bosch halogen headlamp, an
oil cooler nestling under the nose of the tank and
stronger Ceriani front forks, still at 38mm.

The first true development of the 3C came in 1975
with the Slater inspired 3CE – 'E' for England. That
year, Slaters, with rider Peter Davies, embarked on
what was to become a successful racing venture. Armed
with that experience, Roger Slater tinkered with the 3C
to produce the E. The footpegs were raised and moved
back; the standard dual seat was unceremoniously
ditched in favour of a single seat and a Renold racing

chain replaced the usual Regina. The most significant
alteration concerned the exhaust system. Although
visually somewhat similar to the 3C's pipes, those on
the E had undergone serious revision; the baffling of the
3C had been dispensed with, the collector pipe was
bigger and the silencer outlets were larger and extended
from the silencers.

The E's exhaust note was suitably raucous and
decidedly anti-social but was worth 8 or 9bhp at peak
revs. There was little to choose between the 3C and its
successor in terms of power, but the E's top range
acceleration was superior. The E could cover the
standing-start quarter mile in 12.9 seconds and it was
capable of notching more than 140 mph.

Very few 3CEs were built and none by the factory.
Slaters had shown the way, however. Next off the
production line for 1976 was the 3CL that was to form
the basis of the quasi-legendary Jota. The stock 3CL
had moved on from the 3C in that it enjoyed cast
wheels, triple discs and a tail fairing but Roger Slater
perceived a gap in the market for a yet more potent
device. As is well recorded, Jota was not an official
factory name but was Slater's choice, being derived
from a Spanish dance in three-four time.

First made available in the UK in January 1976, the
Jota's engine was fundamentally that of its predecessors
but extra punch was derived from a factory cam profile
and piston shape which had been borrowed from the
works endurance racers. The motor had one function
and one alone: high-speed performance. The racing

ABOVE 'PK' (Pete Davies) and his riding of the Slater Brothers 3C(E) and Jotas perhaps did more for Laverda sales than anything else. In the late 1970s in England he worked the magic; slight in stature, he would be 'shaking the brute' (not the other way around) to the chequered flag. This is Snetterton, March 1976, Avon series, ahead of a 900SS Ducati.

RIGHT The first Jota, 1976 model. Note the famous Jota 'pipes', tail fairing and thin-web Flamm cast wheels with rear disc, with the Voxbell horns mounted on the bottom yoke. In 1976 this was the best sports motorcycle money could buy. No rearsets yet either, Heavy, brutal and too much for many.

camshafts rendered anything less than 3,000rpm purgatory; the tachometer needed to register at least 4,000rpm before the motor sounded even moderately happy, by which point 70 mph was on offer. By 5,000rpm the engine settled down to mechanical sympathy, and the hitherto hesistant, complaining exhaust note mutated to a full-bodied roar. Although the red line applied at 6,500rpm, equivalent to a modest 115 mph in top, the Jota's genuine limit was 8,000rpm, producing a top speed of 141 mph.

The Jota instantly became one of those rare beasts, a 'modern classic' and as such received the accolade of a test in *Classic Bike* in 1980. The overall impression reported was of an immensely strong engine contained in overstretched cycle parts.

Once on test, however, the frame's performance under stress belied this perception, for the duplex cradle, with the single top tube, never flexed under the awesome power available. The frame was harnessed to Ceriani suspension units. Laverda's own cast alloy six-spoke wheels were stopped by Brembo discs that were faultless apart from an irritating tendency to develop unsightly rust at the merest hint of rain. A neat touch was that the footrests, handlebars, gearchange and brake pedals were fully adjustable with benefit apparent in terms of comfort and relaxation.

Only Slaters offered the Jota, at £2,305, in 1977. If that was certainly at the top end of the range, Laverda could probably claim that the machine justified its price tag, for the factory's philosophy was to use the best available accessories regardless of origin; the CEV indicators and Voxbell horn were of Italian provenance, but the speedo and tacho were without apology courtesy of Nippon Denso.

The Jota's lines were almost universally regarded as handsome. There was an elegant three-into-two exhaust system. The paintwork, that was silver and black on the early models, was superb, and even the chrome was passable – both entirely uncharacteristic for Italian machines.

But of course the *raison d'être* of the Jota could be found in the fact that it was in reality almost a production racer. Straight out of the crate, it could take its place on the grid without the owner having to face the daunting prospect of spending hours in polishing heads, undertaking various weight-saving exercises or improving the brakes. In short, it was the finished article.

Admittedly, the nature of the product posed problems for those who wished to unleash it on the open road. The high bottom gear and close ratios, while fine for the track, presented a handicap in town, as did the exhaust note that repelled friendly neighbours and attracted the boys in blue with equal promptitude.

Despite these minor quibbles, the Jota soon attracted a faithful following, no doubt drawn by the mystique of what was hailed as the world's fastest production roadster. A *Bike* review rendered a graphic description of handling the monster: 'To get the most out of it in any situation the rider needs to heave the machine around with plenty of positive body language. Wring its neck down the straight, stick it into the corner, and wrestle the beast down to where you want it. The long wheelbase (57½in) makes the Jota understeer somewhat, widening the line through a bend. Don't worry about that – just pull it down like you had your arms around its neck.'

Only the UK market was supplied with real Jotas. The factory built the bikes, except for the silencers and collector box. All other markets had only 3CLs, although Jota parts could be fitted.

Slaters effected few immediate changes to the Jota; but in 1978 they began importing the Jarama, so named after the racing circuit outside Madrid. The Jarama was the softer-tuned version of the 3CL available to the American market, and indeed Slaters brought these bikes back across the Atlantic from the States. The Jarama had a left-hand gearchange, lower gearing and different carburettors and was finished in either red or green. Although not as distinctive a motorcycle as the Jota, the Jarama was significantly cheaper and hence sold reasonably well.

It will be recalled by Laverda 'tifosi' that Roger Slater, when first importing the twins, had advertised Laverda as 'the Lamborghini of motorcycles.' By chance, Lamborghini had dubbed two of their cars Jota and Jarama in 1970; those who seek for some significance should be assured that this was indeed pure coincidence.

In 1979 there was unveiled what to many enthusiasts qualifies as the definitive Jota: that with silver frame and orange paintwork. The changes were more than cosmetic. New 38mm Marzocchi forks were introduced and the seat was revised. Significantly, reflecting the

The silver-framed Jota with orange bodywork, a 1979 model photographed in 1980. Note horn location, Marzocchi suspension front and rear, rear grab rail and 1200-style frame. Apart from the exhaust collector and silencers all was assembled in the Breganze factory. Looking dated by now. (Tim Parker)

ABOVE LEFT The first Jaramas were American-specification 3Cs of 1976 vintage. This Jarama is later – note the angled rear shocks à la 1200, thick web wheels – almost certainly a 1979 model. Still cable clutch. These later Jaramas were not re-exported back from the USA into the UK but produced specially for Europe and labelled this way for Britain. (Tim Parker)

LEFT 1980 model Jota in England. Now with factory rear-set footrests, new style single seat and fairing that bears some resemblence to that of the 750 SFC. Not many were made. (Tim Parker)

ABOVE 1981 model Jota, much as the previous year but with a new fairing again. The last of the 180 triples was still a good machine if not a great machine – within the series the 75/76 models had to be that, with what was to come next, the 120. (*Motorcycle Sport*)

company's concern for impending noise legislation, the centre main bearings were changed from roller to caged ball type. Indeed, a few decibels were saved but, disastrously, the new bearings had been inadequately tested and after a couple of thousand miles they would break up causing massive and expensive damage to the afflicted engines. This design fault, allied to another in the cast iron skull fitted to the cylinder head, almost signalled the death knell for the Jota as a commercial enterprise in the UK.

Although 1980 allowed the Jota to recover some lost ground, problems still cropped up. New valve springs were weak and displayed a disconcerting tendency to break, while the valve sizes had been increased, with a distressing valve-to-valve contact besetting some bikes. At least there was now the longed-for hydraulic clutch although the pull was still no formality.

The beautiful but troublesome orange and silver Jota entered its final year of production, 1981, with the ignition moved to the primary chaincase, so that the left hand casing now sported a little bulge at the front. This, the last of the first-generation Jota range, underwent an extensive test for *Motorcycle Sport*. The conclusion: 'Any Laverda enthusiast will know that the triple is single minded and never designed to tickover. Laverdas are meant to go. And go it does. It is another of motorcycling's premier sensations, a true horizon eater, highlighted by all the appropriate noise effects.'

Although maybe a legend in its own lifetime, the Jota was by now in danger of becoming seriously outdated, reliant as it was on an engine design that could be traced back to 1973. A major problem, particularly if compared to, say, Ducati's twin cylinder Hailwood Replica, was the excessive vibration generated by the 180-degree motor which featured the two outside pistons rising and falling together producing an uneven firing arrangement. Hence, for 1982 Laverda came up with the more refined Jota 120.

The '120' identified the new crankshaft which had its crankpins spaced equally at 120 degrees, offering equal firing intervals and optimum primary balance. The Laverda engineers surmounted the vibrations posed by the potent secondary forces by using six rubber mounts between the engine and the frame.

Although fundamentally the engine remained unchanged, there were mechanical refinements. The new crank relied on needle roller bearings housed in special sleeves, the oilways were revised, the gearbox was redesigned and the gearchange was swapped permanently to the left-hand side. The triplex primary chain was ditched in favour of two single chains.

Although the 120's engine may not have strayed too far from its predecessor, the new machine could not be

1982 and the last of the line. Similar in looks to the 1981 180 triple, the new 120 – although actually an interim model just prior to the all-new RGS – was a masterpiece. Available in a smoke black-red or bright red, the few machines produced were quickly sold. Note the top rear engine rubber mount. (Tim Parker)

mistaken, as it was clothed in traditional Italian fire-engine red or classic maroon red and boasted a half-fairing with built-in indicators and a new set of instruments.

On the road, the 120 handled better than the 180, although it was always difficult to identify the source of this improvement, as the sole amendment to the duplex cradle frame was the addition of a small brace near the swing arm pivot (although the engine was rubber-mounted).

Phil Todd, whose Motodd concern had been experimenting with a homespun 120-degree Jota in advance of the apperance of the works version, conjectured that improved quality control of the frames in the factory might have made all the difference.

ABOVE The 1950 version of Francesco Laverda's 75 cc machine, with the very distinctive egg-shell tank. (Franco Rossi)

BELOW The 200 cc Twin cylinder machine. This bike, dating from 1962, still lives in the factory in Breganze. (Franco Rossi)

ABOVE LEFT The 750 SF in production from 1970 to late 1972. (Franco Rossi)

LEFT A 1974 second series 750 SFC with Brembo discs. (Franco Rossi)

ABOVE The distinctive 750 SFC half-fairing in Laverda's vibrant orange; 1975 model with electronic ignition. (Tim Parker)

ABOVE LEFT **SFC in unusual but attractive colours, in classic competition. (Don Morley)**

LEFT **1980 1000 Jota, the first with a fairing; the second-to-last 180-engined model. (Tim Parker)**

ABOVE **1984–85 RGA Jota with Sprint bodywork; a special version for the UK by the importer, Three Cross Motorcycles of Verwood, Dorset. (Tim Parker)**

ABOVE LEFT RGS 1000. (Don Morley)

LEFT Early 500 Montjuic in standard street form. Harsh but fast, a great if anti-social sports motorcycle. (Tim Parker)

ABOVE Alan Cathcart, Battle of the Twins, Daytona 1984: a winning combination. (Don Morley)

ABOVE Perhaps the most famous road racing-motorcycle of the 1970s, Laverda's 1000 vee-six endurance. It ran once in the 1978 Bol d'Or 24 hour race at Le Mans. (Tim Parker)

BELOW The endurance racing vee-six. A demonstration run at the factory's tiny test track. (Franco Rossi)

Ground clearance was adequate in normal conditions, with the exhaust pipes and footrests neatly tucked in, although the alternator cover on the right was in jeopardy *in extremis* on the race track. Shod with Pirelli Phantoms, the roadholding was excellent while, as ever, the Brembo discs came in for lavish praise: 'lots of bite and control, no fade and not much lever play', reported *Bike*.

The critical observer could raise an eyebrow, or even two, if he was a fully trained fault finder. First of all, the seat; although visually appealing and comfortable enough for the solo rider, the pillion passenger had to sit on the hump with his head stuck uncomfortably in the wind. A proper dual seat was indeed available but the purchaser had to cough up an extra £86 for the privilege, to add to the standard and already hefty £3,500 – £500 more than the 180 that was still available.

Another gripe was that the Nippon Denso speedo had km/h readings with mph marks that were too small to be of any use. Mirrors were conspicuous by their absence; the generally held theory put forward in defence of this policy was that they would never be required!

The arrival of the 120 Jota coincided with Laverda UK importation shifting from the concern that had become almost synonymous with the marque for UK enthusiasts, Slater Brothers, to Three Cross Motor Cycles, near Ringwood, directed by Keith Davies.

The new importers promptly lent one of the 120s to *MCS*, seemingly confirmed Jota fans. The magazine's complimentary review concluded that the most individual aspect of the bike was its noise and the tester admitted that 'in conscience, we have to say that when returning home to a sleepy suburb at about 10 o'clock or circumnavigating any of the old people's homes that proliferate in our caring community, a twinge of doubt occasionally marred enjoyment of this uninhibited roadburner.'

Sadly, despite the introduction of this handsome machine, the Laverda company was now in deep trouble, so much so that Massimo and Piero were already casting about for the machine's replacement. So it was that the reign of the 120-degree Jota would be but brief. Nevertheless, despite its limited production run, the 120 has duly taken its place in the Superbike Hall of Fame.

Perhaps the attraction of the Jota range was most neatly summed up by *Motor Cycle International* when in 1989, in a retrospective review, the magazine opined that 'in these days of ultra smooth, ultra quiet 16-valve 135 mph middleweights, it's pretty difficult to justify owning a Jota. Not that a Jota is slow or particularly evil-handling, it's just outrageously uncivilised and brutish. And that's its appeal. It's so loud and uncompromising that riding one comes as a breath of fresh air in a nanny state where more and more regulations threaten to take the fun out of motorcycling.'

Not overly slim, the 120 Jota was still relatively easy to ride. Actually it wasn't really a Jota at all with a near RGS-specification engine without even Jota exhausts. Here you can see the modern instruments. Considered by many to be the best Laverda triple produced. (Tim Parker)

CHAPTER 7

Triples in the 1980s

To outward appearances, Laverda passed through the 1970s in fine fettle, with a trail of racing successes and a range of glorious bikes to their credit. In addition, quite apart from the motorcycle division, it should not be forgotten that the Laverda empire embraced a diverse collection of enterprises. First and foremost, the family's original venture into agriculture machinery remained intact in Breganze. In addition, the family had acquired a foundry in Gallarate, home of MV Agusta, that could not only produce motorcycle components but also offered research into sophisticated aircraft and ship design. For instance, the foundry was involved with the production of wheels for the notorious Starfighter. Although one wheel cost a mere 10,000 lire to make, it would cost 60,000 lire to analyse its failure – that would occur after no more than a dozen landings. Finally, the family took to producing caravans.

Despite this wide base, the motorcycle company entered the new decade facing a host of problems, primarily concerned with personnel and the target markets. Undoubtedly a devasting blow was the death of founder Francesco in 1976 and a couple of years later another was suffered when the company's first employee, the faithful Luciano Zen, went into early retirement. To keep his hand in, Zen took up a consultancy with the Ligier concern advising on the construction of invalid cars with Italian motorcycle components. Tragically, he died of liver poisoning shortly thereafter and another link with the past was severed.

In the late 1970s Massimo had engaged Giulio Alfieri as a part-time consultant, most notably in connection with the vee-six project, and when he too passed on to pastures new in 1980 Massimo had to cast around for a replacement. As his successor, Alfieri recommended Giuseppe Bocchi who was an expert in high-revving motorcycle engines. He was an ex-MV Agusta staff man, having worked extensively on the heads of the world championship winning three- and four-cylinder engines and having designed the proposed flat four boxer.

Sadly, at about this time Massimo was afflicted by an illness that left him unable to work for more than an hour each day. This was unfortunate to say the least, for the motorcycle market was being savaged by the world-wide economic recession, with Laverda sales hit as badly as, or worse than, others.

Massimo explained the importance of the export market thus: 'With the twins, we soon obtained a foothold in the USA with Jack McCormack but we were conscious of the risk of being over-dependent on one market and so built up our network of importers in the Netherlands, the UK, France, Australia and South Africa. In the early 1970s, when we were producing, say, 6,000 twins per year, perhaps 60% were exported.

'It was absolutely crucial for us to export our machines. We were exploiting a niche and so could never hope to appeal to more than 2% of potential purchasers. So we needed 2% of a big market and not just 2% of sales in Italy. Also, the Italian mentality is odd. However good an Italian product might be, the Italians will be reluctant to buy it if there is a foreign alternative. They have a craving for foreign goods, perhaps to show that they have emerged from the poverty of the post-war era and are now wealthy.'

At the onset of the new decade, it seemed to the press that plenty of ambitious projects were afoot. For some time there had been rumours that Massimo was planning a liquid-cooled shaft-drive vee-four and in 1982 Piero confirmed that the traditional triples were at the end of their distinguished life. He revealed that the next project would undoubtedly be a 750cc four-cylinder, although whether it would be a vee or in-line had not been determined.

Sadly, the four-cylinder never saw the light of day, as Massimo explained: 'Yes, when Bocchi came to us he designed a four but I put a stop to the project before it really took off as it did not stand a chance. If we had built a four, we could have done nothing other than copy Japanese models. Not only would we have built a copy, but it would probably have been a poor copy, because we simply did not have the resources to match the phenomenal R. and D. departments of the Japanese companies. Finally, once we had come up with our design, it would probably have taken us two years to develop it fully before we could go to the market. In the meantime, the Japanese would have moved on, because they certainly do not stand still; every year they come up with either new models or, at worst, refinements of their existing bikes. So not only would we have produced a poor copy, but even worse it would have been an old poor copy!'

Instead, Massimo believed that Laverda had to

LEFT 1983 and an early RGS. Standing behind, left to right, are Keith Davies of Three Cross Motorcycles (post-Slater Brothers UK importer), Massimo and Piero Laverda. In spite of the somewhat serious demeanour of the Laverda brothers, they had much to be proud of.

BELOW The RGS was extensively tested in 1982 and 1983; much was new and needed it. Here's a factory hack enjoying silence during noise testing in Breganze. Everyone knows just how glorious a Laverda triple can sound in spite of world regulations. (Tim Parker)

1984 American specification RGS engine with, of course differences from the European version. Front mudguard (or fender) side reflectors and exhaust pipe bleed screws to allow for American emissions 'testing'. The American version came with close to a dozen 'necessary' warning stickers; there's one on the fork leg. (Tim Parker)

exploit its own particular niche: 'It would have been nonsense for Laverda to try to compete with the Japanese on their own level. It is necessary for a smaller company to find a tiny opening and to try to appeal to a dedicated band of enthusiasts who will buy their bikes almost come what may. Take Ducati; they have a reputation for desmo twins, have consistently built on that and have cornered the market. The same theory applied to Laverda, and probably still does. We built exciting triples; in truth they were expensive and their performance fell below that of the Japanese bikes in time. But they were original and different, and there are always some people who are happy to buy exclusivity.'

So it was that the ambitious projects were still-born and instead the company continued to rely on the trusty but increasingly old-fashioned triple, in the form of the 1,000cc RGS, RGA and SFC series.

Beset by European bureaucracy, of necessity the company recast the Jota to ensure that its 130-mph plus motor could pass the dreaded noise meter tests. The bike to emerge was the RGS, that was first displayed at the Milan Show in 1981 but did not come into production until the following year. Starting with the 1982 120 Jota engine, Bocchi was called upon to design new cams with the aid of recently introduced computer technology. The consequence was that the power delivery was softened so that there was a steady,

predictable flow from low revs, instead of the sudden urge that hit the Jota at 6,000rpm. And crucially, the RGS featured brand-new silencers!

The frame also came in for some tinkering. The spine was now supported by two tubes running alongside and the whole plot was lowered by a couple of inches, achieved by trimming the cradle around the engine and relocating the Bosch ignition system. The usual components were employed: Laverda's own Campagnolo-lookalike wheels, Marzocchi suspension, Pirelli tyres.

The new bike was bedevilled by too many faults ever to be the marque's much-needed money-spinner. First, and seemingly incredible to a Laverda fan, the Brembo brakes were deemed unresponsive by some testers, particularly in the wet – an implausible criticism as the brakes were unchanged from those used on the 120 Jota. But what was undeniable was that all the controls, and

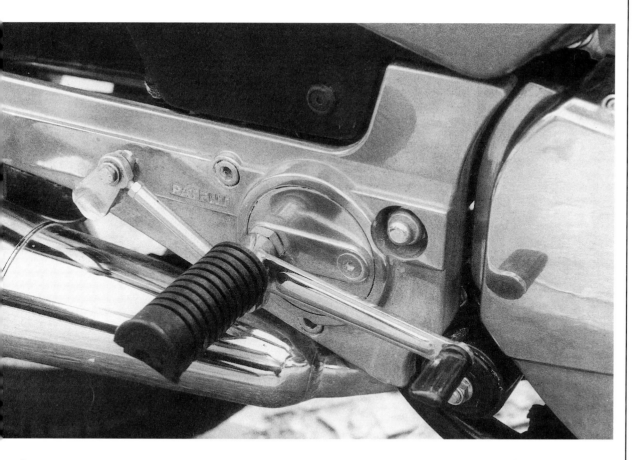

The RGS-range featured these somewhat complex adjustable footrest mountings; visually beautiful and equally well made, they don't have the real adjustment they might. Below the gear lever is a Silentbloc engine mounting; these rubber mounts are effective in dampening engine vibrations: but perhaps the machine was a little *too* silent.

not just the clutch, were uncomfortably heavy; and the gear lever had the unhappy propensity to find a neutral between third and fourth.

The saving grace was the fairing that had been completely redesigned in a more aerodynamic fashion so that the rider's body was well protected from the elements. Just to prove that it is impossible to satisfy all the people all the time, one tester concluded that the fairing was excessively efficient as it encouraged riding too fast for the conditions! Apart from the tank the rest of the bodywork was in Bayflex, a strong but flexible wonder material finished off in a special bright red or silver paint. The pure lines of the tank were undisturbed by an unsightly filler cap. Instead a tube ran through to a flap lurking beside the headlamp, with a lockable cap within.

The company was seeking an upmarket image and

hence the bodywork had been farmed out to RG Studios – that prompted the name RGS. Evidently the attempt met with some success for testers invariably described the machine as 'sophisticated'. One remarked that petrol pump attendants were prompted to refer to an RGS rider as 'Sir', not 'Mate'.

If the RGS was a bike with refined manners it did have one serious drawback. The lack of noise and real distinctive character did not necessarily endear it to the hard core of Laverda fanatics; it was just too bland.

Another of the RGS's defects was its price: a hefty £4,250 in 1983. Accordingly, Three Cross Motorcycles prompted the factory into offering the poor man's version, the RGA at a mere £3,575. The extremely expensive frame-mounted Bayflex bodywork was replaced with an ugly handlebar-mounted small headlamp fairing, together with a new tank and seat.

Over the next couple of years the factory offered nothing very imaginative, merely derivatives called the RGS Corsa, the RGS Executive and the RGA Jota.

Despite its name, the Corsa was not a racing machine but a high-speed tourer, an uprated RGS. Changes were made to the pistons, with the usual flat top pistons scrapped in favour of forged items poached from the factory's Formula I racing bike, so that the compression ratio was upped to 10.5:1 from the standard machine's 9:1. There were other tweaks: the inlet valves rose from

ハイウェイを俺は自慢のバイクで
ご機嫌に飛ばしていた
その横を何かが隼のように
そしてさり気なく抜き去っていった
次のエリヤでそれはすでに
羽根を休めていた。

LAVERDA RGS1000

村山モータース ☎(03) 378-0181／378-2571／377-1182

39.5mm to 40.6mm and the exhaust valves went the other way, from 35.1mm to 34.4mm. The factory was always reluctant to quote bhp figures but the Corsa was rumoured to be almost another 8bhp to the good at the rear wheel at 8,000rpm.

The Corsa also benefited from some new brakes from Brembo: three 280mm drilled floating discs that were regarded as sensitive and powerful if not for the inexperienced or hamfisted. Finished in black, it was undoubtedly a mouth-watering machine but at a price, for it cost a hefty £500 more than the RGS.

The Executive was intended as a sophisticated sports tourer version of the RGS, coming with colour-keyed aerodynamic panniers, but such an exclusive rarity was never going to be the marque's life-saver.

Similarly misguided was the RGA Jota, one of the myriad examples of a manufacturer in trouble hastily resuscitating a much-revered name from the past. For £200 more than the standard RGA, the Laverda buff could arm himself not only with the celebrated Jota name but with an RGA bedecked with lower bars, black pipes and the obligatory orange paintwork.

Perhaps more exciting was the production, in 1984, of a special UK edition, thanks to importer Keith Davies of Three Cross Motorcycles. He felt that there was a gap in the market for a truly hard-hitting sporting

ABOVE If not for the first time with a Laverda, then certainly for the first time with any significance, there was a sales drive for the RGS in Japan. Featuring a factory promotional photograph, Murayama Motors tried very hard. Their advertisement succeeds in showcasing much of what is handsome in the RGS.

OPPOSITE ABOVE 1985 1000 RGS Corsa – in black – without Jota pipes. Note the detailing of the wheels, the Brembo Goldline 280mm floating front discs and FO8 calipers – nothing else to make it a Corsa is visible. A stunningly handsome and effective motorcycle, loved by many.

LEFT In an effort to offer a less costly motorcycle, Laverda developed the RGA 1000 and RGA 1000 Jota (left). The Bayflex fairing and petrol feed system of the RGS was undoubtedly expensive to produce, the fork mounted fairing and conventional tank of the RGA did reduce the price; but it also knocked the appearance for six. The unfortunate front-end styling spoiled an otherwise excellent machine. (Tim Parker)

ABOVE The 1000 SFC; photographed in 1985 in factory grounds with the Dolomites as a backdrop. Lots of cosmetic changes from the RGS/RGA; apart from bodywork there's the footrests, swing arm, wheels and suspension. In reality, it was a more sporting looking Corsa, styled after the factory Formula 1 road racer of a year earlier. The frame is gold, the bodywork red.

RIGHT Three Cross Motorcycles, the UK importer, tried hard to transform the RGA with this fairing designed and produced by Sprint. It was an improvement, although it almost hides the handsome engine totally. This road test machine uses the factory three-into-one exhaust. Orange paint and the Jota name sold some machines. (Tim Parker)

Laverda. Just as Slater Brothers had converted the staid Alpino into the rip-roaring Montjuic, so Three Cross took hold of the RGA Jota and shook it into shape, to produce the Jota Special.

As first impressions are so important, the UK Jota was supplied with an English-made full sports/racing fairing, in orange but touched in black, intended to enhance the machine's looks and prompting an aggressive image.

More importantly for potential customers, a range of engine tuning was available, to cater for road or track use. Modifications included the forged pistons offered as standard on the RGS Corsa, 120 Jota camshafts, a revised airbox and recut and narrower valve seats. The result: a boost in top speed and acceleration above 6,000rpm, albeit at the expense of some mid-range power. A final refinement was available from Slater Brothers, still keen purveyors of parts Laverda, in the shape of an exhaust system for racing purposes. Straight off the factory's Italian Formula I bike, this was a three-into-one affair that in theory enabled the engine to be revved to 9,000rpm and was clearly stamped 'For racing use only'.

The price of the Jota Special was a pound under £4,000 rising to £4,682.98 complete with the engine tuning and exhaust system – interestingly, still less than the Corsa.

The final flowering of the triple came at the Cologne Show in 1984 when the factory launched the SFC 1000: once again there was the suspicion of a hallowed ancestral name being exploited in the forlorn hope of breathing life into a defunct corpse. In this case, however, cynical suspicions were to prove to have been ill-founded, for the new bike was one of some considerable merit.

By 1985, the SFC 1000 was available in Britain and no less an authority than arch-Italian motorcycle aficionado, Mick Walker, testing one for *Motorcycle Enthusiast*, described the bike as 'pure magic' and 'Europe's most exciting motorcycle'.

At the heart of the beast, the motor was undeniably outdated. An aircooled, two valves per cylinder engine with an almost square bore and stroke ratio at 75×74mm may not have won many prizes for advanced engineering but it was sufficient to propel the machine's 538 lb to a top speed of 145 mph. The point was that the Laverda engineers had transplanted the Corsa's tweaked power plant to the SFC. According to *Bike*'s dyno, this motor was good for 84.4bhp at 7,000rpm. Peculiarly, opinions as to the engine's delivery differed violently. Some riders claimed that it was silky smooth; others found the machine difficult to run in town traffic at under 3,000rpm and noticed a flat spot between 4,000 and 6,000rpm.

The cycle parts were very much the recipe as before; the duplex cradle frame of tubular steel, a square section alloy swinging arm (to satisfy the demands of fashion, according to Massimo), top-of-the-range front and rear Marzocchi suspension units and tyres by Pirelli.

Other features were a new fairing, although it was akin to that of the RGS, a 22-litre fuel tank with an electric tap, the familiar Bosch BTZ electronic ignition system and, for stopping the monster, three drilled discs with Brembo Gold Line equipment.

The new SFC was universally well received. Mick Walker found it to be rider-friendly, finding that he could easily get both feet flat on the deck when stationary and that the adjustable clip-ons and footrests enabled him to tailor it perfectly. He also praised the instrument facia, an alloy panel mounted within the fairing, that consisted of a Smiths rev counter, a Smiths speedo and a small Veglia temperature gauge together with a row of five warning lights.

Whereas Walker regarded the handling as agile and predictable, *Bike*'s tester was less complimentary, describing it as ponderous and at one stage going so far as to opine that 'Riding a camel must be like this, though that animal's fuel consumption is better.'

Mike Nicks, then the editor of *Classic Bike*, probably got it right when he wrote that 'The SFC is a rider's machine, for those who don't want their machines to make life too easy'. Lest this be thought to have been a damning review, Nicks offered high praise for the firm suspension, the light clutch operation and the crisp action of the five-speed gearbox.

The factory's original plan had been to build a mere 200 SFCs before launching out into a new range of three-cylinder, middleweight machines. And of this limited edition, a batch of 50 was allocated to Keith Davies who sold out without too much difficulty once it became common knowledge that these represented the last of an illustrious line.

The gold of the frame and the red of the fairing certainly made for a handsome machine but at £5,250 it was no give-away. Another £200 would buy a sports kit consisting of a three-into-one exhaust system, which had a chromium sleeve over the silencer, and larger main jets for the 32mm carburettors. Available for the race track was a package that included revised camshafts, special valve springs, 36mm carburettors and a close-ratio gear cluster.

Although the SFC 1000 had been intended as a limited production affair, it lingered on by reason of the malaise that was to affect the company throughout the second half of the decade. The red SFC was displayed as the flagship of the range at the Milan Show in late 1987 together with a black machine, shod with wire wheels instead of the standard cast 18in versions, aimed at the German market. Even as Nuova Moto Laverda got underway in 1989 there were tales of further SFCs being built, essentially to use up old stock and bring in some much needed lire. What a sad and poignant conclusion to the marvellous career of one of motorcycling's most celebrated three-cylinder engines.

RGS: Tim Parker

I once asked Massimo Laverda what RGS stood for. He answered me with a twinkle in his eye, 'Real Grand Sport'. Is this bike worthy of that? Unlike most Laverdas which instantly commit one to an opinion, the RGS leaves many including me unsettled. On the positive side I like the looks very much, although frankly, the fuel filler system which contributes strongly to the style (because of the smoothness of the tank top) is a mechanical nonsense adding unnecessary weight and complication and much cost. Further, the Bayflex bodywork is a lovely idea but I don't know of one case where its ability to actually flex has saved anyone pain, only created more. The adjustable footrest system has so little adjustment in it that it too is almost worthless, although technically I like the idea. The single/dual seat concept I also like but the actual seat is devoid of comfort after 50 miles. These four characteristics make an RGS; underneath it is, of course, a 120 Jota but without the Jota. The Corsa brings back the Jota element to the RGS but the other criticisms don't go away.

Yes, I like the RGS and certainly enjoy riding my own now that I have softened the damping front and rear and played a trick on the seat. I can only conclude that it was never developed sufficiently. In a way the Corsa was no development at all and the 1000 SFC went in a different direction (not to succeed there either). The RGA was a step backwards, a lesson in taking away what visual character the RGS had and replacing it with a Honda CX500 'flying maggot'-style facelift in an attempt, I assume, to save cost. 'Real Grand Sport', yes, close but not a bullseye.

The RGS Executive was essentially an RGS, usually in a silver paint obtained from BMW, with handlebar fairings, higher bars and streamlines panniers. It deserved to do much better on the showroom floor than it did. One reason it didn't was that the panniers didn't carry enough and didn't have sophisticated mountings — unlike BMW.

1,200cc

When in the mid-1960s, Massimo launched his family company into the production of large-capacity machines, he was following the American maxim that 'big is beautiful'. But, sadly, ten years or so later, the marque's flagship triple, the Jota, was a non-starter in the States. It was simply too difficult to market, in part because it was too sporty; and its gear shift location and exhaust emission did not satisfy American legislative requirements.

Massimo's response, and his final attempt to pierce the USA market enjoyed by Harley-Davidson's 1,300cc monsters, was to add an extra pot onto the 750 twin to produce a 1,116cc triple and call it, somewhat cheekily, a 1,200. The bike that emerged in 1978 came in three basic versions: the quiet, docile, standard model available worldwide, its companion the TS, clad in a nose fairing and side panels and finished in silver, and the jazzed-up variant exclusive to the UK, the Mirage.

In these hard times, the prohibitive costs of a new design simply ruled out anything innovative and hence the new bike was based on the 3CL. First of all, the bores were enlarged by 5mm to 80mm thereby extracting another 135cc. But the designers had not been content to rest at that. In particular, new flat-topped pistons were introduced and the compression ratio was down to 8:1. The vertical parallel triple breathed through the same 32mm Dell'Orto carburettors used by the 3CL. The estimated 85bhp at 7,000rpm took the bike to 131 mph on a road test in April 1978.

The modifications to the engine had been intended to retain the triple's fearsome power while ensuring that it was more manageable at high revs, in keeping with the bike's tourer image. The 1,200 indeed shed much of the Jota's aggression so that the machine was more stable and comfortable but there remained its essential character. The engine still used the 180-degree crank favoured by the earlier triples and with the pins so set the two outside pistons ran in unison firing on alternate strokes. Hence vibration was a noticeable factor. However, when *Bike* magazine took a big triple to the Isle of Man for a test during TT week, it challenged some Laverda owners on this point and they responded that it was a positive boon as the vibration made them feel that they were riding a 'real motorcycle'.

The full loop frame remained basically unchanged from that of the 3CL but the trail and wheelbase were increased slightly, in part through steeper angled rear shocks. Standard suspension was by Ceriani but Slater Brothers offered De Carbon gas-filled shock absorbers as an optional extra while later 1200s emerged from the factory with Marzocchi units. The cycle parts could certainly handle the triple and *Bike* judged it thus: 'You *could* find better handling bikes – like the Ducati Super Sports which after all is the ultimate in ultra-fast cornering, but for the versatility of its roadholding characteristics the Laverda takes a lot of beating. As a high-performance sports bike it makes a very passable tourer. Over the low speed town running and long motorway hauls where out-and-out sportsters like the Ducati can really crucify you, the Laverda rider stays cool and comfortable.'

Other features of the 1,200 model were the familiar Nippon Denso switchgear, Bosch electrics, twin Fiamm horns, cast alloy five-spoke wheels, two Brembo discs at the front and one at the rear, and the three-into-two exhaust system of the 3CL. The $4\frac{1}{2}$-gallon fuel tank offered a range of 150 miles, and was bedecked with stick-on decals instead of the usual tricolour Laverda badge. The standard bike, that came in maroon or blue, was initially priced at £2,550.

Lest it be thought that the 1,200 was fault-free, a *Motor Cycle News* test drew attention to the extremely heavy clutch action and the fact that the five-speed gearbox suffered from a distinct 'notchiness' and emitted a heavy 'clank' on a gearchange. The TS sported a new look with a special fairing, deep engine and below-seat side panels and seat. It came only in silver.

However, in the UK, Laverda fans were not really interested in a humble tourer, even if it was a wolf in sheep's clothing. They craved the genuine article, and to satisfy this appetite Slater Brothers came up with a specification for a 'Jotarised' version, the Mirage. Taking the standard bike, modifications included lower bars, culled from the 500cc Alpino, revised cylinder head and pistons, endurance race cams, a re-designed air filter and Jota pipes. Additional novelties were drilled disc brakes, hydraulic clutch, new instrumentation and switch gear and a re-styled bodywork complete with a nose fairing.

The Mirage, selling initially at £2,695, soon became the best-selling Laverda in the UK thanks no doubt to rave reviews from the journals. For instance, *Bike*, seemingly dedicated Laverda buffs, commented on the

LAVERDA MOD. 1200 "TS"

FOTO VAJENTI VICENZA

1981 factory studio shot of the 1200 TS. This one is for the Italian market; there were changes for other markets. Note the primary drive cover change; hidden from view is the hydraulic clutch. Marzocchi rear shocks are now fitted as are the thick web cast wheels. Both hydraulic clutch and thick web wheels came in 1979. Standard suspension on early 1200s had originally been by Ceriani.

Dated November 1977, an early 1200 in the factory grounds. The white seat wasn't productionised. Still Ceriani forks and up-front horns. Stick-on tank decals and graphics. Note the angle of the rear Ceriani shocks.

LEFT Roger Winterburn, now a Motorcycle shop proprietor, was once an employee of Slater Brothers. Here he demonstrates a Formula Mirage (1200).

RIGHT The first 1200s were usually plum red or metallic mid-blue; the Mirage usually a vivid green. The 1979 30th Anniversary 1200s were always black with a gold frame. Note the subtle changes in the equipment – drilled front discs, Corte e Cosso rear shocks and new style petrol taps, and the crude '30th' designation on the tank. Up until this model, Laverda's reputation for excellent finish was intact.

BELOW Slater Brothers' road test Mirage at Bromyard in 1978. Now Marzocchi front forks but with Ceriani rear shocks and the familiar side horn mounting position. Mirage was UK-market Jotarised-1200 with obvious Jota silencers. The mirror is probably ex-Kawasaki. (Tim Parker)

Mirage: 'Like the Jota, it's a magnificent red-blooded sports roadster that'll out-perform and out-handle almost anything else. But it has a greater suppleness of suspension, more relaxed riding position and low-speed torque that makes it a lot easier on you around town and over long distances. ... It's so beautiful it deserves a place in a gallery somewhere as an example of the fusion of aesthetics and functionality that seems a uniquely Italian engineering flair. The motor is a blend of beautifully finished, highly polished die castings, and hunks of matt-grey sand cast alloy, made at Laverda's own factory.'

In their search for the ultimate, Slater Brothers went one step further and produced the Formula Mirage, strictly for the discerning and wealthy enthusiast. This was the Mirage clothed in a sinuously-shaped tank-seat unit inspired by the Italian Motoplast concern and bejewelled with gold Astralite wheels, black exhausts and Brembo Gold Line brakes.

In 1979 the 1,200cc triple entered yet another incarnation in the form of the Anniversary, a limited edition purportedly issued to celebrate the marque's thirtieth birthday as a motorcycle manufacturer. Cynics would have it that it was merely a crude marketing device to get rid of unsold stock!

The Anniversary was nearer the standard model than the Mirage, for it did not possess the tuned engine, and in truth it had moved on but little from the original 1,200cc bike. Its principal selling points were the cosmetic touches that were unashamedly intended to catch the eye. For some time, salesmen and marketing men had been convinced that black and gold were the colours to sell bikes and Laverda reacted accordingly. The Anniversary's paintwork came in black and nothing but black while the frame and cast alloy wheels were duly gold. Gold stripes lined the fuel tank, seat unit and front mudguard.

The price was certainly hefty at £3,095 but the Anniversary enjoyed a half-fairing, drilled Brembo discs and a hydraulically operated clutch that was a distinct improvement on the cable-operated version on the standard model.

Underhand and gimmicky it may have been, but the marketing ploy worked and the Anniversary was soon sold out. *Motor Cycle News* had no difficulty in finding faults with the bike but nevertheless advised, in words entirely in keeping with Massimo's philosophy, 'Buy one tomorrow and love it for what it is and what Japanese bikes aren't.'

Whatever criticisms could be levelled at big Laverdas over the years, and there were a veritable multitude, in general they exuded character, style and charisma. The 1,200cc range was no exception and *MCN* duly concluded their road test with the chilling words: 'If looks could kill, the Laverda Anniversary would be wanted for mass murder'.

CHAPTER 9

Seventies miscellany

Although of relatively small significance in the annals of the Laverda saga, for the sake of completeness a brief mention should be made of four virtually anonymous – to English enthusiasts, at least – machines that emerged from the Breganze stable durng the 1970s: in chronological order namely the 250cc Chott, the 2T/R of the same capacity, the 125cc Regolarita and finally the quarter-litre steed of the same name.

The first of the quartet, the 2T, 'due tempi', otherwise the Chott, was for some obscure reason named after a Tunisian lake and made its bow at the Milan Show late in 1973. Powered by a 250cc Laverda-designed two-stroke motor, it was one of the first middleweight Italian machines intended for a combination of road use and off-road ventures – and cynics claimed that it succeeded in neither function.

The prototypes underwent extensive testing in the early months of 1974 and the bike emerged in a thoroughly modern guise, boasting delights such as electronic ignition, a dry clutch, enclosed final chain drive and variable rake. An abundant use of lightweight materials contributed to an estimated 20% weight saving, yet surprisingly the mudguards and tank were steel affairs and the total weight was 260 lb.

Visually, the machine could charitably be described as disquieting. To make room for the bulky exhaust pipe, the engine was placed high in the duplex tubular frame which actually relied on two sets of top tubes. The inelegant exhaust pipe, the large saddle and the protective covering around the chain made for a none too pleasing overall impression.

In fairness, there were some neat touches. The crankcase, finished in a resplendant gold, was treated with three coats of a special protective paint to counter the rigours of off-road use. The frame, which consisted of small-diameter tubing, boasted variable geometry, with three different settings available at the steering head. The saddle could be removed easily, as it was secured by two bolts, to give ready access to the air filter that had been thoughtfully mounted well away from any flow of dust and muck. The plastic side panels were simply pressed on to three rubber mounts and behind the left-hand panel sat a 12-volt battery. Behind its right-hand counterpart was the Bosch ignition system and a tool bag complete with an instruction book.

The aircooled engine, with piston controlled porting, was square at 68mm for 246cc, and produced 26bhp at 7,600rpm. It was fed by a Dell'Orto 33mm carburettor and delivered power via a five-speed gearbox. Other features were the 11-litre petroil tank, which included a 3-litre reserve, Ceriani suspension units and Metzeler tyres, 3 by 21in at the front and 4 by 18 at the rear. By request, Metzeler Six Day covers could be fitted.

The Chott, when thoroughly tested by *Motociclismo*, was damned with faint praise. The riding position, although generally comfortable, was badly let down by the poorly placed controls. Both handlebar levers were awkward to operate and in particular the lights switch on the left-hand bar was too far from the grip for ease. Similarly, the gear lever, on the left-hand side, bore no obvious relationship to the foot rest. A serious defect was that the front drum brake, a 180mm magnesium offering by Laverda, although adequate in off-road use, failed rapidly on tarmac.

The final indictment related to the handling, although it was necessary to read between the lines of *Motociclismo*'s tester's report. He noted that the engine hiccuped below 3,000rpm and recorded that it ticked over quite happily on the couple of occasions when the machine was dropped!

A handful of these machines come to Britain and one of them was tested by *Bike* in 1977. Its performance in mud was declared unexceptional: 'With its trials pattern tyres offering minimal off-road grip, any attempt at rapid riding just resulted in a fountain of muck from the rear wheel and no appreciable increase in forward velocity'. The Chott suffered from the failing of a close-fitting mudguard so that on the test the mud became wedged firmly between the tyre and the guard with the inevitable consequence that the wheel stopped turning!

The point was that the Chott was not a pukka enduro bike; it was designed, with its efficient lights and instrument complex, to give a degree of roadgoing comfort and utility that a serious competition machine would have eschewed. Of course, in so doing, rather than embracing both the off-road and roadgoing disciplines, it merely fell between the proverbial two stools. Nor could the Chott claim to be attractively priced. Imported by Slaters it was available at £840 whereas for instance the Kawasaki KT250 was on offer at a modest £615, to fulfil the identical role.

The next offering from Breganze along these dispiriting lines was an updated Chott, a sporting version called the 250 2T/R – 'due tempi regolarita'. The

TOP It's late in 1973 and Laverda announce their first 250cc two-stroke called the Chott. On paper it looks good, in the flesh it was a little overweight. Its development cost must have been enormous. That 180mm mag front drum brake came in for some serious criticism.

ABOVE With the fuel tank removed one could study the adjustable steering head. The bottom bolt was the pivot, with the three adjuster holes at the top. Unfortunately, the Chott needed more power and less weight before a steering and suspension improvement could come into effect. (Dave Minton)

The Chott featured a healthy rear drive chain case that gave full enclosure, and a large seat. It wasn't all bad; in this case too much, too late. (Cycle World)

advances on the original were scarcely noteworthy: a
reinforced frame, plastic mudguards and Metzeler Six
Day tyres as standard. The new bike was stripped of its
predecessor's instrumentation and given a number of
cosmetic refinements: a black engine, red frame, white
tank with red markings and white mudguards.

The 30bhp engine was regarded as the 2T/R's strong
point, being sufficiently tractable and forgiving to
extract the careless rider from a self-induced mess, with
quite exceptional acceleration available in the lower
gears. Sadly, Laverda had not corrected the mistakes
perpetrated on the Chott; the control levers and pedals
had been simply lifted from the Chott and remained
less than functional. Weighing 250 lb, the 2T/R
suffered from an excessively high centre of gravity and
was generally regarded as too cumbersome to be ridden
comfortably for long spells. A combined production
run of 5,000 for the Chott and the 2T/R told its own
unhappy story.

The Italian dealers were, however, anxious to offer
lightweight machines to supplement the big twins and
triples. They pestered Massimo to produce smaller
capacity bikes to ensure that their showrooms were full
with a wide range to suit all tastes and pockets.

The marque's continued involvement in the off-road

**The next development was the 2TR, in 1976, the only
obvious changes being the high front mudguard and
the tank graphics.**

market stemmed from its association, as importer, with
the celebrated Swedish Husqvarna concern. At the
time, Husqvarna enjoyed a splendid reputation in the
sporting arena and produced two very lively 125cc and
250cc two-stroke engines. Massimo came to a deal with
the Scandinavian company whereby these motors were
supplied for the Regolarita models.

The eighth-litre bike appeared at the end of 1975 and
was tested in competition throughout the following
season by the national moto-cross champion Italo
Forni.

At the heart of the matter was the reed-valved
aircooled 123.6cc Husqvarna engine with 55×52mm
bore and stroke dimensions. The Swedish company
traditionally declined to reveal power outputs but it was
disclosed that the Laverda technicians, led by engineer
Sandro Todeschini, extracted another 3bhp with their
modifications that raised maximum revs by 500rpm to
10,500. Todeschini tinkered with the reed valve in

A new model for late 1976 was the 125L/H for Laverda Husqvarna. In this prototype, the radial head Husky engine still features its 125CR label.

order to improve a hitherto lacklustre performance between 2,500 and 3,000rpm. He also replaced the 32mm Bing carburettor with a Dell'Orto for two reasons: one, logistics, in that the latter company was on hand to proffer assistance; and two, efficiency, for the Italian carburettor performed better at high revs. Also featured were Bosch plugs, a six-speed gearbox, gear primary drive and chain final.

The tubular frame, weighing 28 lb, was based on the latest Husqvarna moto-cross steeds, duly revised on the recommendations of Forni after his competitive endeavours. It sported a single diagonal top tube, with two smaller diameter horizontal tubes alongside and one tube at the front running down to the triangular-shaped bottom tubes. Marzocchi forks were employed at the front with the same firm's inclined gas units at the rear. 3 by 21in Metzeler moto cross tyres were chosen, together with 140mm Grimeca drum brakes.

The machine went into production in the spring of 1977. Although the company then pulled out of official participation in moto-cross events, a fair quantity of the models were sold to privateers who performed nobly in numerous lesser events throughout the peninsula. A section of the competition workshop at the factory was devoted to the 125cc Regolarita with Todeschini heading a team of mechanics whose principal task was to support the privateers.

The second Italian moto-cross championship round at Leffe was the scene of an extensive test of the bike in the hands of the *Motociclismo* squad. The engine was regarded as 'robust' and was particularly commended for its power and tractability at low revs while the handling was up to standard on all terrains. Two particular problems were noted: first, the clutch was none too smooth; second, the gear ratios left much to be desired.

The bike, finished in SFC orange, was attractive enough, although the elegance of its lines was perhaps diminished by the excessive gaps between the cylinder head and the tank – a necessary evil to facilitate plug removal – and between the rear wheel and the mudguard.

All in all, the 125cc bike was a tempting package. Its price, 1,308,000 lire, put it amongst the lowest of its

ABOVE 1977 250 Husqvarna-engined Laverda in Breganze, Looking quite modern and more Husky than Laverda, a good number were made and sold. Laverda's two-stroke off-road effort deserved to do better. (Dave Minton)

LEFT 1977 and a final fling. The cycle parts of this enduro 125 looked in keeping with the obvious guts of the Husqvarna engine.

kind, while its top speed of 73 mph was a shade slower than the Ducati Regolarita but faster than similar products sold by the likes of Gilera, Fantic, Mondial and Puch.

Laverda had negotiated an exclusive import agreement with Husqvarna for the 125cc motor and there was a logical progression when it was extended to cover the 250cc engine in 1978. Hence, an enlarged Regolarita rolled off the Breganze production lines: the 250cc version was dubbed the LH2 – Laverda-Husqvarna.

The machine differed from its progenitor in detail rather than principle. Bore and stroke dimensions were 69.5 × 64.5mm for 244.7cc and the engine breathed through a 38mm Mikuni carburettor. Somehow the

information leaked out that maximum power was 28bhp at 7,750rpm.

The suspension, generally regarded as excellent, retained Marzocchi units at the front but Corte e Cosso inclined units, with five settings, were favoured at the rear. Tyres were by courtesy of Pirelli, with a 3 by 21in at the front, stopped by a 140mm Grimeca drum, and a 4 by 18in at the back, matched with a 160mm Grimeca.

The 250 was priced at 1,679,000 lire as against what had risen to 1,467,000 for the 125 – thanks to the perils of inflation.

Reading the test reports of the 250, its merits and defects seemingly bore scant resemblance to those of its smaller sibling. It was damned as suffering from excessive vibration and unacceptable noise, particularly when ridden fast on the road, whereas the 125 had received high praise in these departments. By contrast, the clutch now came in for extravagant plaudits for its ability to endure the most savage treatment. The Husqvarna quarter-litre engine earned top marks for being ultra responsive, its only apparent failing being that it was a poor starter in both hot and cold weather.

Ultimately, however, the test that matters is that of the market place. The stark truth was that little more than 2,000 of the Husqvarna-engined models were sold in a three-year period. Laverda had simply been barking up the wrong tree.

CHAPTER

Alpino and Montjuic

Laverda's foray into the 500cc market commenced with the production, in 1977, of the Alpino that is today regarded by most marque enthusiasts as a relatively lacklustre model. Nevertheless, within a couple of years this dowdy machine had been transformed into the distinctive and undeniably classic Montjuic.

Rumours of a 500cc machine had been rife in 1974 and so it was no great surprise when a prototype twin-cylinder model was shown to the press in September of the next year. After a lengthy gestation period the Alpino hatched but in truth it did not appear to be anything startlingly novel. Instead, it followed the lines of the 750s in that it was an air-cooled transverse parallel twin, albeit with chain-driven dohc valve operation. Like its predecessors the engine was slightly inclined and reminiscent of the Honda CB72/CB77 range. The motor was typically Laverda with its clean lines and horizontally split crankcases. It featured bore and stroke measurements of 72mm and 61mm respectively for a total capacity of 497cc. Wet sump lubrication was employed, and Dell'Orto PHF 32 AD carburettors.

The gearbox had the boon of a sixth gear but most testers regarded the extra gear as a luxury rather than a necessity. The clutch was wet multi-plate, the primary drive by gear and final by chain.

The frame was a single loop welded all-steel affair which split into a duplex engine cradle and sprouted a rear sub-frame. Front forks and rear shocks were both by Marzocchi, the latter five-way adjustable. The wheels were Laverda die-cast aluminium of the five-spoke variety and tyres were Pirelli Mandrake, at 3.25 × 18in. Brakes were Brembo discs, double at the front and single at the rear.

The electronics were courtesy of Bosch with the alternator serving a 12-volt battery and the German concern also supplied a potent six-inch quartz halogen headlamp. The Nippon Denso instruments were easy to read. The Lanfranconi silencers came in for unusual praise in that they were handsomely chromed. The seat was lockable and concealed a first-class array of tools in a detachable tray. Footrests and gearchange and brake pedals were all adjustable.

The Alpino's dry weight was 374 lb and in its original style the machine was finished in a pale blue with a black frame, although red, green and orange paintwork soon became available. For some, the stick-on label

LAVERDA on the tank was a tacky touch.

How did this scaled-down 750 fare? The new gearbox generated universal praise with a sweet change. The engine was distinctly edgy beneath 3,000rpm and it was not until 5,000rpm had been attained that a sense of ease pervaded the powerplant.

Suspension and roadholding were also regarded as creditable, with a more precise handling available than on the 750s. The brakes, in time-honoured Laverda fashion, were simply the best. The only adverse comment was that the cast iron discs displayed a disturbing ability to turn to rust after the merest hint of rain.

Within twelve months, Laverda had improved the package to produce the Alpino S, which boasted a number of refinements paying homage to the great god 'Performance'. Higher compression pistons were fitted and a rotating counterweight was added at the left-hand side of the crank to smooth out the inevitable vibration of the twin.

A new colour scheme was on offer: black with gold stripes, in the manner made fashionable by the JPS Lotus of Formula One fame. Neat little touches identified the machine: the chrome plated footrests; the frame welds, which were well concealed and neat; rubber mounted silencers and headlamp; and even a small oil bottle in the toolkit.

Although the factory was fairly coy about revealing statistics, 44bhp at 9,500rpm was a realistic estimate, and a six-speed gearbox allied to a dohc affair driving four valves per cylinder should have been a hot package. Tested by *Bike* magazine, it was reported as producing a top speed of 100 mph prone, or 91 mph sitting up.

The major problem, in the UK at least, was the prohibitive price tag: £1,675. The similarly performing Honda CB400 was on sale for a little over half the price, the Honda CX500 vee twin cost £1,207 and even Yamaha's shaft-drive 750 triple was cheaper than the Alpino.

But as *Bike*'s tester Graham Sanderson pointed out: 'You have to realise that any biker in the market for the distinctive brand of motorcycling offered by Laverda isn't likely to endure sleepless nights working out the price versus performance versus capacity equation.'

The Alpino was aimed at the eccentric with a passion for 'real' motorcycles with gorgeous Italian styling and built-in exclusiveness and who, it must be said, was

TOP 1977 model 500 twin. Primary side cover shows no balance shaft yet. This style is still close to the original of 1975. The basic specification didn't change much: double overhead camshaft, four valve and six speed.

ABOVE The UK-market 500 Alpino S with the altered primary cover to accommodate the balance shaft. Otherwise not much change from the 1977 model, except for tank graphics. Sales were never strong.

ABOVE **Glorious line-up of the Formula 500s at the factory. Note the one-piece tank and seat unit. There was a second production run with a separate tank and seat, although still to a similar shape. They made a good, basic road racer.**

LEFT **A line-up of 350 twins at the factory awaiting crating for shipment. Tank badge indicates the date is likely to be late 1979 or 1980. Not a fast machine. (Motorcycle Sport)**

prepared to pay through the nose for the privilege. Thus the Alpino's true competitors in the UK were not the ubiquitous Japanese mass-produced machines but the 500s produced by Ducati, Guzzi and Morini, all of which at about this time were offering charismatic vee-twins.

Although contemporary road tests were charitable, with the benefit of hindsight the overall impression is that the Alpino's performance, looks and character were simply not up to standard and hence the bike never did carve a niche for itself in the middleweight market.

Twelve months after the launch of the Alpino, Laverda came to the market with a 350cc version. This move had been prompted by the fact that machines below 350cc enjoyed a reduction in the Italian equivalent of VAT, with a consequent saving of about £200.

The cycle parts were merely poached from the 500cc model while the motor was a scaled-down affair, with

the bore being reduced from 72mm to 60mm which with the stroke of 61mm gave a displacement of 344.5cc.

The dohc assembly was still driven by a central chain but the inlet valve sizes were reduced by 3.5mm to 23mm and the exhaust valves by 4mm to 20mm. The Dell'Orto carburettors were now 24mm versions. The compression ratio went from 9.2:1 to 8.7:1, but as usual Laverda did not disclose the bike's power output.

Testing the 350 in September 1978, *Motociclismo* raised a number of criticisms. The footrests were too high, causing fatigue on a lengthy journey. The tester found the machine difficult to control in town as the gearchange was none too cooperative at low speeds; and the final black mark was that acceleration left a lot to be desired. On the credit side, the sweet and progressive clutch, the sportster-like handling, the forgiving suspension and the potent and tireless brakes were all to the good.

The Breganze twin had a top speed of 96 mph, compared with the Morini 350's 100 mph and the Guzzi V35's 89 mph. It was no lighter than its 500cc stablemate (typical of a scaled-down motorcycle), and hence paid the penalty of being heavier than both its most direct competitors: but it did enjoy the advantage of being considerably cheaper than either of them, selling for 1,277,000 lire as against the Morini's 1,871,880 lire and the 1,898,100 lire of the Mandello product. Despite all those seemingly impressive statistics, the machine never really caught on. Only 683 were built over a five-year period.

On Saturday 11 March 1978, the Breganze factory hosted the launch of 75 500cc twins based on the Alpino

but race-converted for use in the forthcoming season's single-marque championship, dubbed the 'Formula' version. The 'Coppa Laverda' was a promotional race series running from March to October with three rounds at Misano and one at each of Imola, Pesaro and Mugello.

The series was open to riders under the age of 30 who had never before been placed in the top three in any race. The sports supremo of the championship was Laverda's Sales Director Giuseppe Tagliolato and Luciano Zen was the technical overlord.

Assisting Laverda in this project were other leading trade names such as Pirelli, IMOS Italia of Turin who provided Phantom crash helmets and Total who supplied the fuel and oil.

The Formula 500 was 35 lb lighter than the standard road bike, thanks to the removal of the accessories required for street use and the fitting of a lightweight single-piece tank and seat. (A purchaser did however receive a box which contained all the pieces required for a street-legal conversion, including registration documents.)

The engine was modified in a number of respects.

The pistons were slightly heavier than on the stock bikes and the compression ratio was 10.5:1. The power came in at 6,000rpm and maximum output was 52bhp at 9,500rpm. As with the Alpino S, a rotating counter-weight was fitted to smooth out what would otherwise have been an unbearable vibration at higher revs. Riders were permitted to modify the seat and the jetting, but that was it.

Before one of the rounds at Misano the *Motociclismo* testers got their sticky fingers on one of the race bikes. They were impressed by the handling, stable despite the fact that the frame and suspension were standard items coping with a significant increase in power. The sole complaint in this area was that the front wheel had a tendency to feel light in fast curves. The journalists were, however, rather sceptical about the claimed top speed of 125 mph and judged that the bike lacked punchy acceleration.

The Formula was offered to would-be (or more likely never would-be) Agostinis complete with a dolphin fairing that a cynic might have viewed as little more than a running billboard for the series sponsors, whose stickers abounded. But it was really no more than their

ABOVE The second series Montjuic with Motoplast style bodywork. At least the fairing was properly mounted this time. Today a very rare version and getting more valuable all the time. (Tim Parker)

LEFT Everyone loved the Montjuic, at least the first ones, though perhaps just to look at. Fast, frantic and anti-social on the street, they were an expensive toy. The handlebar mounted fairing accounted for a certain amount of wobbling on the track. Harshly tuned they could prove fragile when over-revved, something they encourage the rider to do all the time.

due for their input. There was some modest space reserved for the riders' personal sponsors, unless they happened to be in competition with any of the official series promoters.

Of course, at each round the helmets, fuel and tyres were provided by the promoters and Laverda sent along a lorry absolutely bursting with mechanics and a vast supply of spares. In keeping with the nature of the series, the price of spares was kept to a minimum; for example, £15 for a piston, £25 for a fairing, Pirelli tyres at £15.

The initial package was very reasonably priced, at a touch under £1,500, which was actually very little more than the Alpino's price in Italy. Laverda certainly cannot have made a profit from the sale of the Formula machines but they stimulated tremendous interest and requests for the steed came from Spain, France, the Netherlands, Belgium and West Germany. Indeed, there was a development of the bike, featuring a separate tank and seat, and a race series was held in West Germany.

Slater Brothers, at the time heavily involved in production racing, obtained a Formula 500 and Roger Slater was quick to realise that therein lay the ingredients for a truly distinctive sportster. The result: one of the all-time classic Italian motorcycles, the Montjuic, so named after the parkland circuit in Barcelona which hosted the endurance races in which the Laverda half-litre models met with some class-winning success.

The Montjuic was in essence a refined Formula 500 and as a racer let loose on the roads it was instantly

The last attempt to build a saleable and rideable 500. This is a red 500 Sport of 1984, first conceived for the Spanish market. Not much had actually changed from the Alpino S of five years earlier. Sales in Spain were fairly healthy, elsewhere less so. This one is in the factory showroom in Breganze. (Tim Parker)

identifiable, both visually and audibly. Visually, it looked fast: a one-seater with sports handlebars, a little flyscreen fairing, a pair of tucked-in matt black megaphones, finished in a conspicuous fiery orange. It sounded fast; if the Montjuic had to be described by one word it would have to be 'noisy'. All in all, the Montjuic was a unique device and comparisons with other motorcycles are simply pointless, invalid.

The bike's appearance certainly generated enthusiasm. The first series seat and handlebar fairing

able joints posed as clip-ons hiding behind the nose-cone, which had small screwed-on sections to deflect air past the hands.

To deal first of all with the shortcomings of the Montjuic, it must be admitted that they were numerous, although in the main, petty. The tiny fairing, although successful in easing the rider's lot, was initially fork-mounted and was generally believed to contribute to a weave that beset the machine at speeds over the ton. Accordingly, many of these models were soon shorn of their nosecones. The second series fairing, inspired by the Italian Motoplast concern but once again manufactured in England, was slightly larger and protruded under and alongside the tank and was adjudged altogether less sensitive, being frame-mounted.

The scantily padded seat was another source of complaint for, when combined with an unrelenting rear suspension, even on the softest of its five settings, an uncomfortably hard ride was assured.

In typically Italian fashion, the finish was not all that it should have been. Disgruntled owners moaned that the sidecovers were soon stained in streaks where the unfiltered Dell'Orto carburettors coughed out petrol spray while the front mudguard and orange paint enjoyed no more than a brief acquaintanceship. Peculiarly, considering the extensive effort that had been made with the Alpino, the exhaust pipes' black paint was also a temporary arrangement.

Finally, the switchgear was awkward, the Nippon Denso speedo optimistic and the tachometer misleading. This last instrument was red-lined at 8,000rpm, but maximum bhp was not attained until 9,000rpm and the engine would run smoothly at 9,500rpm.

The reputation of the Monty has always been that it will come to life only at more than 80mph, that in traffic and beneath 6,000rpm it is just plain difficult, that it has to be constantly blipped at traffic lights and in jams and, above all, that it bellows out the most raucous cacophony imaginable with a violently anti-social exhaust note. All of this is true, but the Montjuic was intended for the individual who was not over-concerned with his neighbours' eardrums, who would not be tootling down to town to do his shopping and who would be motoring at speeds such that the lack of rear view mirrors was an almighty irrelevance.

The Montjuic's natural habitat was on long, sweeping, undulating roads, mimicking the racetrack that its progenitor the Formula was built for. Contemporary road tests reveal that speeds of well over the ton could be held indefinitely on motorways, that 300 miles could be gobbled up in comfort, and that the Monty would devour country roads with an alacrity matched by few of its contemporaries of whatever capacity.

The bike was low, with a seat height of 29in, and had a dry weight of 360 lb, so that it had the feel of a 250cc machine. The light weight, the relatively wide section tyres at 4.10 × 18in – and the Brembo discs – combined

were made in the UK by Screen and Plastic and their lines, when allied to those of the steel tank and the glassfibre tail, created the desired image of the street racer. Incidentally, the tail featured a semicircular lower edge, no doubt intended for the racing number!

The footrests were mounted up and back on neat alloy plates which sat within the triangles of tubing that on the Alpino S were to hold the pillion footrests. Needless to relate, the Monty did not contemplate passengers. The goosenecked 'Jota bars' with adjust-

to stop the machine in a surprisingly short distance, in keeping with the best Laverda traditions.

Some interesting statistics of the Montjuic and its major competitors as at August 1980 are as follows:

Machine	bhp/rpm	top speed/mph	UK price/£
Benelli 504 Sports	52/8,900	106.7	1,999
Ducati Pantah	46/8,500	119.1	2,299
Morini Maestro	46/7,500	105	1,735
Montjuic	50/9,000	106.4	2,295

The now defunct *Motor Cycle Enthusiast* magazine, quite a fan of Laverda products, undertook a thorough comparison of the Monty and the Ducati Pantah on the basis that, as Italian sports bikes with café racer styling, they were superficially alike. The conclusion of the back-to-back tests was, however, that the two machines were actually fundamentally different. The Ducati, for all that it was regarded as a civilised commuter-cum-tourer, was castigated as a compromise; as an attempt to enter a Japanese dominated market, it was bound to fail because it was inevitably priced way beyond the equivalent machines from the oriental giants.

By contrast, the Montjuic, while limited in many and indeed most respects, earned full marks as 'an out-and-out sports bike' being 'of little use for anything else. It would be virtually impossible for commuting because of the harshness and inflexibility of the motor. It is built for either the club racer or the rider who is well-heeled enough to own a bike or car for riding to work and can use the Montjuic for a mind-blowing hour or so on an evening or at weekends.'

As one perceptive reviewer put it, perhaps crudely but certainly appropriately: 'it's best ridden after you've pulled your brain out and left it in a safe place.'

Co-author Raymond Ainscoe and his wife contemplate life with an ex-Phil Todd Mark I Montjuic.

The Slater-inspired Montjuic met a premature end, being savaged by EEC noise regulations imposed by that universally despised clique, the faceless bureaucracy of Brussels.

Production of the 500cc motorcycles ceased in 1982, for the very good and proper reason that by then a loss of £750 was suffered on every model made. The company persevered with sales of the Alpino but merely to clear old stock, not as a serious money-spinning project.

The standard machine was the Roadster that was finished in silver or black and was available in the UK in 1983 at a price of £1950 from Three Cross Motorcycles. The Sport, in red, cost another £50. Originally intended for the Spanish market, the Sport offered a slightly higher compression ratio than the Roadster but differed essentially in cosmetic touches only. It boasted narrow clip-ons, a nose fairing and, as an optional extra, rearset footrests, all of which were intended to enhance its sporting image.

In fact, the Roadster and Sport machines were generally dismissed by testers as but humble Alpino derivatives, best described as beneficiaries not of the Montjuic's charisma but, in the completely justified words of *Motorcycle Enthusiast*, of 'standard issue Laverda flip-up/fall-over spring-loaded sidestand.' Production figures in 1981 and 1982 of 170 and 100 respectively told their own sorry story; and the company's first foray into the middleweight arena came to a predictable conclusion.

Riding the Montjuic: Raymond Ainscoe

Visiting Phil Todd to chat about matters Laverda, I espied in his garage a mouthwatering fireball – a real live Montjuic. My fingers twitched, my resolve to consolidate my bank balance wavered and when the astute Phil muttered 'I really think you should buy it,' I could only agree.

A fortnight later I was back down in Surrey, complete with trailer and a fistful of hard-earned and easily dissipated notes, to collect the beast. 'Er, you do know it's noisy?' questioned a concerned Mr Todd. Yes, indeed, I knew all that. I had read all the road tests of a decade ago.

Well, forget the written word and second-hand opinions. You have to sit astride a Montjuic to savour its unique charms and qualities, although on reflection perhaps 'charms' is barely an appropriate word for this, arguably the most uncompromisingly embarrasing anti-social two-wheeled device it is possible to ride on the public highway.

Perhaps I am over-sensitive, conditioned by living in Ilkley which is a genteel, civilised sort of place, well populated by a mix of octogenarians and golf-playing executives. But just as soon as the Monty was fired up, I had more than a sneaking suspicion that the bike's appearance would not be greeted with universal enthusiasm by the local worthies.

First port of call – a mistake indeed – was the centre of town. Arriving at the first set of traffic lights barring the Leeds-Skipton road I found out for myself that, as reputed, the fearsome engine did not idle. Pressing the starter button kicked the 500cc motor into an almighty racket, marginally less noisy than a 747, prompting a host of wretched Saturday-morning shoppers to turn round to study this orange mini-Jumbo. Thank heavens for the anonymity of full-face helmets!

OK, so the Montjuic is not for town use, but once on some of the gorgeous sweeping quiet roads that lead northwards into the Dales the machine came into its own. My usual companion over those undulating roads is a virtually contemporary rival, a 500cc Guzzi Monza, a sweet-tempered twin-cylinder machine that makes for effortless riding. Now the Montjuic was not quite as much fun, probably because its extra power demands a little more concentration and restraint, but it was far more manageable than I had expected.

I suspect that I was prejudiced against the bike's handling simply because it resembles an unforgiving monster. The engine block is solid and looks uncompromising and, at least by the standards of the 1990s, there is no styling worthy of the description. Nevertheless, once on board the Montjuic, it is actually reasonably well behaved.

On its first appearance, some criticism was levelled at the bike because of its lack of mirrors. I think that this was unjust; I was quite content to look over my shoulder whenever necessary. Nor did I have any complaints about two other bugbears, the seat and the suspension. I did however find one particularly irritating fault. The footrests protruded excessively, so that I found it virtually impossible to put my feet down without clipping them or my calves against the ends of the pegs. True, only a minor defect, but one that I found to be very annoying after a while. For all that, the Montjuic is a unique motorcycle. Thanks, Phil, and, yes, it was noisy.

The Montjuic on test with Raymond Ainscoe, losing friends the easy way. At ease on open roads, difficult in town, but always ear-shattering.

Eighties miscellany

Sad to relate, the lightweight and middleweight products of the Breganze factory during the 1980s were never going to leave the competition agog and, in retrospect, hardly set the pulse racing. Nevertheless, for the sake of completeness, their tale must be told, although a Laverda fan may be well advised to avert his gaze.

At the bottom of the range, the company first entered the 50cc market with the LZ, ie Laverda-Zundapp, available early in 1981. In fairness, the LZ50 was a well-proportioned scaled-down motorcycle, and not one of those uninspiring – to Anglo-Saxon eyes at least – mopeds so beloved of Italian manufacturers. Although less than *avant-garde*, and at some distance from the forefront of styling, the LZ looked both functional and handsome. Visually, at least, it must be adjudged a modest success.

The powerplant, courtesy of the German Zundapp concern, was an aircooled two-stroke, measuring 39 × 41.8mm for 49.9cc. It relied on a Bing carburettor, a Bosch magneto and a four-speed gearbox. The frame consisted of a single top tube with a duplex cradle, with conventional suspension and 17in tyres stopped by 120mm drum brakes. The seat, although at first glance seemingly catering for a passenger, was in fact truncated by the baggage carrier, as Italian road regulations stipulated that 50cc machines could not carry passengers. A Sport version was also on offer featuring a tiny but nicely styled nose fairing. The machine came in for fairly lavish praise from *Motociclismo*; the gears were forgiving, the engine vibration-free and the ride comfortable.

When Zundapp inconsiderately collapsed, Massimo Laverda turned to Minarelli to power the replacement 50cc steed, the Atlas. It came in off-road styling, that had become, by 1985, almost obligatory for any company anxious to tap into the fashion-conscious teenage market. The machine's lines were ample, thus ensuring that this tiny motorbike could be readily mistaken for a 125cc machine – another well-worn marketing ploy.

The Minarelli water-cooled two-stroke 49.6cc engine, with bore and stroke dimensions of 38.8 × 42mm, relied on a 12mm Dell'Orto carburettor and a 2% automatic mix. The cycle parts were nothing revolutionary. A single top tube sprouted into a square section cradle, and suspension was by Marzocchi at the

front and a single Sebac shock absorber at the rear, with a so-called Soft-Ramble system. Tyres were by Pirelli, 21in at the front and 18in at the back.

The bike was quite striking. The black of the engine unit contrasted with the white frame and the metallic finish of what was actually a plastic engine tray.

The *Motociclismo* testers found the Atlas to be an acceptable compromise for both off-road and town use, and praised the braking, roadholding and the four-speed gearbox. Black marks went to the hard gear-change, the machine's excessive height that required a rider to be at least six feet tall before he could put both feet on the ground, and the fact that the engine was straining until 6,000rpm were reached.

A derivative for purely off-road use was the Adventure that differed only in cosmetic detail when it was displayed at the Milan Show in 1987. Of course, by then the commercial enterprise was merely limping along, and production figures for the Atlas of 990 in 1986 and 280 and 230 in the following years tell their own pitiful story.

Although commercially reasonably successful, the marque's 125cc offerings did little to enhance its reputation as a manufacturer of quality machines of mystique and charisma. Massimo Laverda was first ensnared into the ultra-lightweight market when he visited the Zundapp factory in Munich and emerged with a deal that guaranteed him exclusive use of their high performance two-stroke engine. From 1978 to 1983, when Zundapp ceased production, almost 20,000 LZ 125cc models were churned out of the Breganze plant.

Massimo had correctly identified a winner in the water-cooled engine, that was square at 54mm for 123.6cc and relied on a Mikuni 28mm carburettor, a 2% mix and a five-speed gearbox. When *Motociclismo* conducted a comparative test of eleven 125cc machines, the LZ stood out as the only water-cooled engine in use by an Italian factory. The motor offered 17bhp at 7,600rpm and the Italian journal awarded it full marks for acceleration allied with silence, a reasonable fuel consumption and a lack of vibration.

Sadly, the testers thought that the Italian cycle parts were not up to the engine's high standards. The riding position was castigated; the saddle was too high, the handlebars were too low. Accordingly, it was difficult to maneouvre the machine. The frame was nothing too

ABOVE There was a '50' market, mostly for mopeds, scooters and step-throughs, in Italy. Zundapp had an air-cooled 50 engine in their range; hence the LZ 50. This one was nicknamed the Pippo. Years are hard to identify; probably 1981.

LEFT Laverda's OR 50 Atlas (OR for off-road, presumably) was a little but lively mini-bike with a water-cooled two-stroke single. A typical assembly of proprietary parts that might come from any one of two-dozen Italian manufacturers.

ABOVE 1978 Laverda LZ 125. Zundapp's two-stroke single, water-cooled and 5-speed, was an excellent engine, a good choice for a starter/sports bike. Laverda made a neat frame, gave it Italian as opposed to German styling and ensured that it handled and braked well. These weren't fast, but they weren't poor motorcycles for their home market.

RIGHT It was the 125 market that all of Italy concentrated upon. There was no real place in the late 1970s and early 1980s for a 175. Here's one of many attempts to produce a 'sport' 125. Neat little handlebar fairing very like the bigger models, together with rectangular indicators and the blackening of many previously silver or chromed parts, attracted some buyers. Note the Zundapp logo still on the engine case.

elaborate, being a simple tubular duplex cradle affair with Marzocchi suspension units and Dunlop 2.50 × 18in and 3.00 × 18in tyres front and rear respectively.

A Sport version was available in red, boasting a handsome nose fairing, a sleek twin saddle and a price tag to match: 2,127,000 lire as against, for example, the 1,540,000 lire of the Honda CBX as of October 1978. It should also be mentioned that Laverda offered the LZ 175 powered by Zundapp's 163cc engine; it was simply the 125cc model bored out to 62mm.

With the demise of the Zundapp concern, Massimo was forced to seek alternative engines and he eventually decided that the solution was to build his own. Hence,

the next series of 125cc steeds was the LB run – i.e. Laverda Breganze – production of which commenced in 1984.

The homespun engine did not depart too radically from its Teutonic forbear. With the same dimensions, it did actually look like an aircooled 250 rather than a water-cooled ultra-lightweight, thanks to the extensive finning. It was inclined at 25 degrees and relied on a 28mm Dell'Orto carburettor, a five-speed gearbox and gear primary drive.

The engine was slung beneath a slim tubular frame, although there was actually a fairly substantial top tube. Marzocchi front forks, Sebac rear shock absorbers, Pirelli tyres and a single Brembo front disc completed

the specification. Some attempt was made to clothe the machine in fashionable mode, for as well as the by now customary handlebar fairing, the sides of the radiator were shrouded.

As with the LZ, a Sport version was available, although it may well be that the specifications of the various models during these years were none too precise as parts appear to have been used up without over-much concern for adherence to the supposed requirements of a particular model.

One rogue 1984 white LB Sport found its way to London Italian specialists Moto Vecchia. The story of this singleton refugee was quite fascinating. It was purchased in Florence by an itinerant Australian who rode it to London and then sold it to Moto Vecchia to finance his return flight. A report in *Bike* simply enthused over this Sport's distinctive qualities, and in particular its tiny but smart fairing and removable tailpiece over the passenger seat that gave the impression of a baby RGS.

The magazine's test concluded with the words: 'The Sport has already been snapped up by a wealthy Italianophile publishing magnate planning to find its lost horses.' His riding impressions of the machine can be found at the end of this chapter!

The LB also brought the factory some publicity when the Trofeo Laverda was launched for aspiring young racers in 1985. A batch of identical LB 125s was available for the six-round series, with two heats and a final at each venue. Laverda put much more into the

ABOVE **Hard to tell the 175 from the 125 . . . this is a 1979 LZ 175. A few steps beyond the previous machine are front fork changes, inviting you to fit a second caliper (but no way of fixing a second disc!), black indicators, rear shocks and tank badges. (Tim Parker)**

RIGHT **Amadeo Perrone, 27, heads a field of young hopefuls in the Laverda 125 series, 1985.**

series than merely providing the bikes, as Amadeo Perrone, the son of Continental Circus participant Gianni Perrone, explained: 'The competition was an excellent and thorough introduction to racing. Quite apart from the races, Laverda sent all the participants off to a race school at Mugello for a course covering the theory of racing, the proper lines to take and so on. We were also given some mechanical tuition and a set of leathers and a crash helmet.'

The 1985 version, the LB Uno, featured square tubing and in 1986 three more LB derivatives were introduced, the Custom, the Sabbia and the GS Lesmo. The Custom, or CU Ride, was an Americanised model that had undergone substantial cosmetic changes, boasting the seemingly outdated round tubing of the LB that was somehow more in keeping than square tubing with the desired effect, plenty of chrome and an entirely re-shaped petrol tank on which was emblazoned an eagle incorporating the usual Laverda badge.

LEFT The voluminous 125 entry level market in Italy is fickle: demanding, or being persuaded it wants, sports bikes, customs, enduros and repli-racers at a moment's notice. Here's the LB 125 Custom of 1984/85. Regretfully mistimed, although still a reasonable motorcycle. There were several custom versions, one in a desert hue and called the Sabbia (sand).

Ridiculously high bars and a seat to match rounded off the bike.

Motociclismo was moderately complimentary about the Custom suggesting that its hideous Yankee appearance actually disguised a particularly sporty steed, with notable acceleration allied to exceptional brakes and stability.

A couple of years later, the Custom underwent a major re-styling. Simultaneously, the Sabbia was on offer. It was akin to the Custom but was sand-coloured, hence the name, and was equipped for desert riding, in theory! However, by then the factory was well and truly in the grip of its death throes and it was never going to find its salvation in a range of over-priced 125cc bikes relying on fancy styling.

The marque's contemporary effort, the GS Lesmo, launched at the Milan Show in 1985, was so named after the famous curve on the Monza circuit. A mere 2,250 were produced between 1986 and 1989. Could the profit on those machines have covered even the design costs?

The GS Lesmo was intended as a simple sportster with a new square tube frame, the Soft-Ramble single rear shock suspension system and a new six-speed gearbox. It also came fully clothed with a comprehensive fairing that was now absolutely *de rigueur* for any self-respecting sports machine.

The Lesmo certainly had its strong points, thanks to the extra 2bhp that the engineers had squeezed out of the motor, the ease and comfort of riding and, consistently a feature of the marque's products, the unrivalled excellence of the braking, that relied on two Brembo discs at the front. Although the product may arguably have been quality, it did not offer value for money, being by some margin the most expensive of the Italian eighth-litre motocycles. Whereas Aprilia's offering was pitched at 3,550,500 lire (why the 500 lire, about 25p?), and Gilera's stylish RV came at 3,617,500 lire, the Lesmo weighed in at an exorbitant 4,488,000 lire.

A final development of the Lesmo was the GSR, shown in Milan in 1987 with an even more comprehensive fairing, in best Ducati Paso fashion; but the problems besetting the company denied it a fair crack of the whip, so that it never entered serious production.

For years there were unsubstantiated rumours of a middleweight machine just around the corner, ready to break new ground and save the floundering company. One such design did actually see the light of day, for however brief a period: the 350cc L-shaped triple.

Laverda's next real change came with the GS 125 Lesmo in 1986 – why Lesmo was chosen, a corner on the fast Monza track north of Milan, is unknown. Its monoshock with 'Soft Ramble' rear suspension and plastic disc wheel covers outshone the competition to start with, but with trouble at the factory, Cagiva, Aprilia and Gilera took over.

This fascinating departure was a water-cooled reed-valved two-stroke, with cylinders one and three lying almost horizontally while cylinder two sat atop and between them at 90 degrees, in a compact and rigid structure. Each cylinder measured 52.4×54mm, for 116.45cc. The three carburettors sat snugly together above the horizontal cylinders.

A prototype was shown in Milan in 1985 featuring an aluminium twin spar frame and a fairing akin to that of the 125cc Lesmo, with which it shared a single rear shock absorber and the name. At the front came a 16in wheel, whereas the rear was an 18in affair; two 280mm Brembo discs were fitted at the front with a single 260mm version at the back.

The 350cc engine produced 53bhp at 7,800rpm and Giulio Franzan, by then the company's commercial director, revealed to *Motociclismo* that Laverda proposed to bore out the cylinders to 60mm to produce a 458cc motor that would offer 75bhp at 8,750rpm. It was intended that the 350cc machine would be sold as from the following autumn at a price of about 7,000,000 lire but the dream was never realised.

Also in evidence at the Milan Show of 1985 was the OR 600 Atlas, Laverda's contender in the middleweight enduro market, looking for all the world a clone of the OR 50 Atlas. The engine was an improved 500 Alpino unit, a dohc four-valve twin-cylinder plot, with bore and stroke of 76×63mm, a revised lubrication system, a single twin choke horizontal Dell'Orto carburettor and six-speed gearbox. The quoted power output was 50bhp and top speed about 105mph.

The white painted frame was a mixture of round tube and square section tube and contrasted vividly with the black engine that sported six barrel fins with a polished edge as a highlight. The forks, wheels and swinging arm were all finished in gold and the tank featured a black, white, red and blue flash on the sides.

The Spanish-made wheels had Pirelli trail tyres and were both stopped by Brembo single disc brakes. Suspension was courtesy of Marzocchi, with the Soft-Ramble monoshock unit in use. Clocks and switchgear were by CEV. A production run of 300, 60, 40 and 50 in the four years beginning with 1986 speaks eloquently of the lacklustre market performance of the machine.

The OR 600 Atlas was a real motorcycle; it might have been a great enduro motorcycle if money and time had been allowed for its development. The familiar 500 dohc, 4-valve twin was out to 571.6cc, was six-speed still, fed by a twin-choke Dell'Orto carburettor. More significant was that the engine cooling system was improved. Sensibly, the electric starter was retained.

Riding the LB 125: Tim Parker

Back in 1983 and 1984, Moto Laverda was a sales leader in the seemingly lucrative street 125cc market. For a very short time their LB 125 Sport, at a glance a miniature 1000 RGS, was the Italian teenage male's 'have to have' motorcycle. Outside Italy we knew nothing of this, all we saw was disaster looming. Inside the Laverda factory they had a success on their hands. Why?

Frankly, at the time the LB 125 was the most stylish sports bike available and sports bikes as opposed to trail bikes were still the fashion leaders in the fickle but large market. 25,000 units in a year from one manufacturer wasn't a dream. This time Laverda had it right for not only did it look the part but it could play it too. Here was a water-cooled, five-speed Laverda-built (except for the Zundapp barrel) two-stroke single with about 18 horsepower in a very decent tube chassis with colour matched cast wheels and a front disc brake. Easy kick start was a reality and so was 80mph. Automatic lubrication was given.

And this time it was a real motorcylce, in fact it could be criticised for being a little big for a 125, but again Laverda had it right – there was room for a sixteen-year-old girl on the back as well.

I have owned an LB 125 for six years now and travelled some 5,000 miles on it. Perfectly reliable, very comfortable and really quite fast and, outside Italy, perhaps unique.

What went wrong? Unfortunately Laverda missed the next trend, which was street-legal motocrossers with electric starters.

1984 Laverda LB 125. The Zundapp name has gone with only the barrel still supplied for the first models from Germany. (Soon Zundapp was to close down.) Laverda spent much time and money refining their 125 two-stroke with worthwhile results. Unfortunately, progress wasn't maintained. This LB 125 Sport is dressed up for the monomarque racing series. Apart from the expansion chamber exhaust, the major visual differences from stock are the extended rear side panels to the rear and the headlamp cover.

Riding the GS125 Lesmo: Phil Todd

This machine was one of Italy's top sellers in its class. Dealers who ran out of stock often had to wait three months for more. The young Italians loved its up-to-date looks and would eagerly pay more for this machine than for those offered by Laverda's competitors.

Outside of Italy, the Lesmo remained virtually unknown. The high price, and the various power restrictions that some countries imposed, made sure of that. A few made it to the UK, imported independently by dealers. The test machine belongs to Ray Sheepwash, currently the editor of the International Laverda Owners Club magazine, and a well-known Laverda enthusiast, owning four different Laverdas.

I have ridden Lesmos before, not for more than a few minutes at a time, but I had the chance to ride this one for a few days. It is a 1986 model with only 3,000 miles on the clock. The colour is officially described as 'anthracite and white'. The anthracite is actually a very attractive metallic black.

Using full choke, the machine always burst into life with one or two prods of the kickstart. Engaging the first of the six speeds was a noiseless affair but revs were required in abundance on pulling away, to avoid stalling. After half a mile or so the choke could be released by reaching down and lifting the lever that is attached directly to the Dell'Orto carburettor.

The whole geabox operation was a joy. Just as well, as it was necessary to go up and down it like a yo-yo to keep in the narrow power band that is inevitable on a performance 125cc two-stroke. I must admit that I found it hard going at first, but the bike sort of took me over and I found I began to ride with the urgency that this type of machine requires if you are to maintain a good speed.

Each bend required a spot-on choice for the exit gear, otherwise acceleration was useless, and each overtaking manoeuvre required far greater judgement than on the larger machines I normally ride. In fact, I enjoyed riding in traffic immensely, popping the odd wheelie and powering away whilst in the power band. The whole effect was like riding your first bike all over again and it started to turn me into a sort of geriatric delinquent.

On the open road, it felt happy cruising at a shade under 70mph. Vibration was minimal and the excellent mirrors remained virtually blur-free. The stability at all speeds was impeccable. The forks coped well with the bumpy road surfaces that are now part of the British way of life but, on the most horrendous of potholes, the top of the fork slider would hit the fairing. This also happened under severe braking but a heavier fork oil would soon cure it.

Speaking of brakes, they are miniature Brembos. The front stoppers are tremendous, with a progressive action that inspires confidence straightaway. The rear brake was good also, as it would take a great deal of pressure on the pedal to lock the wheel, just the way I like a rear brake to be on any road bike.

The cornering was superb. I am sure that I could have taken every bend at twice the speed that I did; I just cannot seem to adapt to such a light bike. On right-handers the exhaust would just kiss the ground and would possibly cause the serious scratcher some grief. The rear suspension is well matched to the front, making the whole machine responsive and controllable when flicked about at speed. It never bottomed out the whole time I had the machine and fortunately did not require adjustment, as it looked a bit of a pain to do.

The motor is a gem. It is so quiet mechanically, especially considering that it is not working very often below its power band, which is from a shade under 7,000rpm to 9,000rpm. The oil consumption is minimal and the water level never changed. In fact, the whole quality of the machine is top class.

For use as a second or fun bike I would have no hesitation in recommending a Lesmo. With values of rare or unusual machines steadily rising, it could be a bit of an investment too!

Laverda expert Phill Todd puts the Lesmo through its paces.

Specials

Being idiosyncratic motorcycles, with an ardent following of slightly off-beat enthusiasts, it is hardly surprising that Laverda engines have formed the basis of a host of eccentric one-offs and specials, both for street and track. Arguably, the Montjuic and Jota models, inspired as they were by importers rather than the factory, should be regarded in this vein, though they were actually built in the factory.

A list of the craftsmen who have turned their attention to accommodating a Laverda twin or triple reads like a 'Who's Who' of top-notch frame builders. In a more or less extravagant style, Motoplast, Hossack, Spondon, Egli and Harris (to name but a few) have produced their own interpretation of exactly what is required to harness the Breganze horses.

But if there is one man who is noted for his affinity with the marque and the specials he produced for nearly a decade, it must be Phil Todd. A heating engineer by trade, and a motorcyle aficionado by inclination, in the late 1970s Phil found himself tiring of the increasingly irritating fallibilities of his BSA Rocket 3. Not quite desperate enough to turn Japanese, his choice fell upon a 1974 Laverda 3C, reputedly formerly the property of the comedian Dick Emery. Seeking a clutch cable for his new bike, Phil wandered innocently into Morphy Motorcycles, fell into conversation with Colin Morphy and before the day was out found himself in fresh employment there, dealing with a wide range of Italian bikes.

In 1978, Phil returned to Mitcham and, together with another ex-Morphy man, Martin Routley, set up Motodd, to service and deal in machines. There was no clear business plan or direction. Be that as it may, within two years they had been appointed as official Laverda dealers and had moved to semi-underground premises in Croydon.

Phil Todd's entry into the world of conversions and racing came in 1980 when he was approached to build a Formula One machine powered by a Laverda triple – because of course in those days there was a 1,000cc limit. Phil also knew that the factory was planning a 120-degree triple but, as it was not yet available, he made his own. He admitted that the task was fairly simple: 'We just turned the crankshaft, put on new cams and provided a special ignition – easy'. The engine received rave reviews in the motorcycling press, much to its originator's pleasure as he readily appreciated that

impartial press comment was far more convincing than bought advertising space. Phil was also particularly amused, because he regarded his engine as rough and lumpy.

Nevertheless, duly encouraged, he decided to install his creation in a specially commissioned monoshock frame, that although may be conventional by the standards of the 1990s was fairly *avant-garde* at the time. Phil originally proposed that two of these frames should be made by Nigel Hill of Leatherhead but before the first had even hit the streets, visitors to Phil's premises were so impressed that orders for another five had been taken.

Shortly thereafter, Laverda's own 120-degree triple made its appearance and so Phil's engine work ceased but his specials still trickled out, as a flagship for his business as a dealer, spare parts supplier and specialist repair centre. He had a faithful band of customers, some of whom were so devoted to his products that they would update their Motodd Laverdas whenever the next specification was available, going through the range of Mark I, II, III and IV.

By the mid-1980s, somewhat disillusioned with what was emerging from Breganze, Phil realised that the marque was most likely to find a desperately needed niche in the burgeoning classic scene. He reasoned that the young lads of the early 1970s, who had craved for but never been able to afford the unattainable SF

ABOVE RIGHT **Fritz Egli's big-bore tube spine frames have been designed around many motorcycle engines including three from Laverda, the 750 twin, the 1000 triple (featured here) and the 500 twin. Most famous for his Vincent V-twin frame, the Swiss had long had a relationship with the Slater Brothers and perhaps this was his initial reason for making a 750 frame. Few were made to any configuration; there's only one report as to whether it improves handling and that's not proven.**

RIGHT **Motoplast of Italy designed both a frame and bodywork for the Laverda triple with an early attempt at a space frame. Again, few were made and it was not wholly successful in its effect or appearance.**

ABOVE **Motoplast inspired the Slater Brothers creation, the 'Formula' 1000 or 1200. This one is a Formula Jota 120; any number of combinations were offered for the custom customer, all based on the one-piece tank/seat unit. This one has Astralite wheels, three-into-one exhaust, Brembo floating discs and Gold Line FO8 calipers.**

RIGHT **The Harris brothers of Hertford, England 'converted' their Magnum frame designed around Japanese four-cylinder engines to fit the triple. Here's a neat early triple with early steel swing arm. Astralite wheels and aluminium tank probably save enough weight to have made the whole exercise worthwhile. (Tim Parker)**

models, were now company executives and professionals with cash burning a hole in their pocket; in a word, 'yuppies'. This upwardly mobile class was Phil's new target audience, and he set about building a 750 racer to advertise his wares in the increasingly popular classic racing scene.

One afternoon in 1987 changed Motodd's destiny: a customer's RGA backfired, the fuel tank blew up and the fire spread to the workshops. Although the fire brigade put out the flames, there must have been undetected smouldering timbers or papers and during the night the conflagration set in for good and burnt out the premises. The inevitable squabbling with the loss adjusters did little to improve Phil's equanimity.

Shortly thereafter when a customer and a consortium of friends made an offer for the business, Phil and Martin accepted. Martin Routley retired to Hertfordshire and a new career while Phil intended to dabble in racing. However, such was his reputation

within Laverda circles that he was soon being asked to prepare SF engines for a band of loyal customers. Finding himself unable to resist dabbling in importing quality as-new Laverdas and still dealing in spare parts, Phil once again found himself on the treadmill, dealing as Todd Laverda.

However, the Motodd name still lives on in Croydon, under its new ownership, offering the Mark III and Mark IV specials. Indeed, one of the latter achieved some fame, or more accurately notoriety, in the motorcycling press in 1990, described in one journal as a 'no-holds barred loony bike'.

The Mark IV was certainly unusual. Wrapped around the 1,200cc triple was an immensely strong nickel-plated steel tubular frame with an unusual suspension system, courtesy once again of Nigel Hill of Saxon Racing. Although at a passing glance the front suspension looked like a conventional telescopic arrangement, more detailed study revealed that the

sliders, via a ball-joint, triangulated arm and linkage, actually relied on a combined spring and damper unit housed beneath the engine. In previous one-off commissions, Saxon Racing had placed the springing above the engine but with the tall Laverda triple it was more convenient to place the springing unit low down.

A rising-rate rear suspension was also employed by Saxon, while the wheels were Astralite 18in front and rear, with twin Brembo 300mm discs at the front and a single 280mm at the rear. The headlamp fairing and the tank and seat unit were elegant and eye-catching.

On test, LJK Setright was in no doubt that the special steered delightfully at all speeds and on all surfaces, with precision and stability. A review by *Motor Cycle News* endorsed those comments but noted that the bike was less than agile. However, the Motodd Saxon Laverda was surely not aimed at the commuter but, in the very best of Laverda traditions, at the discerning enthusiast with an eye, and a pocket, for the distinctive and charismatic.

The Saxon was not the only Laverda to enjoy experimental suspension. Difazio hub-centre steering appeared on a number of machines. Jack Difazio's system offered a number of advantages over traditional forks; it was possible to govern the degree of anti-dive, wheel movement was substantially upright so that the wheelbase was constant and the trail could be readily altered to suit a rider's preference.

The most celebrated application of this system on a Laverda was with the endurance racer of the 1970s run by Mead & Tomkinson, the south-west motorcycle and car group. One partner, Mike Tomkinson, was an engineer with an affinity for motorcycles, as were his sons Chris and Patrick.

They had run Velocette and BSA singles to good effect in international endurance racing and wanted to move upmarket with a Ducati desmo vee-twin. However the Bologna concern, oblivious to the team's hitherto impressive record, showed no interest. So it was that, with Slater Brothers almost on the doorstep,

A dealer special, the Cropredy Liberator was a triple with an Italian designed (and made) fairing and seat unit similar in configuration to that found on many a Moto Guzzi Le Mans and in style to the Ducati MHR. This is sometimes known as the Cico fairing.

ABOVE A good racing (or street) frame is hard to construct around the massive 1000/1200 triple engine. This is Spondon's try. The Derby, England, racing frame maker's attempt of 1983 was particularly effective, except in making a wide motorcycle even wider. Note the position of the swing arm pivot, right in theory to pivot in line with the gearbox sprocket, but impractical from every other point of view. (Tim Parker)

ABOVE RIGHT Motodd made several brave and sometimes successful attempts at creating a frame to suit the characteristics of the triple engine. This is a development bike which might be described as the Mark 2, photographed in May 1984. Founding father Phil Todd commissioned Saxon Racing to create a monoshock front and rear, and worked at it. The Mark 4 is quite a machine.

RIGHT Road 'n' Race Show in London in 1984, a Harris-Laverda 1000 (late 180 engine) shares a stand with Sports Motorcycles of Ducati fame (Steve Wynn with beard). Chrome-moly Reynolds 531 tubing makes a unique frame, which makes a nice, if not great, sports bike. (Tim Parker)

Mead and Tomkinson developed two centre hub steering Laverda triples in the mid-1970s. This is the second one with Norman White aboard. An innovative but perhaps over-complicated approach.

Mike Tomkinson sought a liaison with Laverda, obtaining an enthusiastic response and a potent triple.

For a couple of seasons the team raced a virtually standard triple, with minor modifications intended to enhance reliability and comfort. But for 1976 the Tomkinson machine was startlingly different. There was no conventional frame. Instead its function was fulfilled by the engine to which, via aluminium plates front and rear, two sub-frames were attached. At the front was a Difazio-inspired unit employing hub-centre steering and a pivoted fork. At the rear, the conventional swinging arm was replaced by a parallelogram suspension offering constant chain tension.

The M & T Laverda, when fitted with its comprehensive streamlining, was undeniably heavy at 480 lb, as against a mere 370 lb registered by the Bol d'Or-winning Egli-framed Kawasaki of Godier and Genoud in 1974. The riders soon discovered its drawbacks. Most unnervingly, it was difficult to judge braking precisely because of the lack of front end dipping. Furthermore, at very high speed the machine's aerodynamics left something to be desired, so that instability set in at above 140mph.

Against that, the racer was fast. Neil Tuxworth, celebrated TT exponent and latter-day manager of Honda Britain, rode the bike at Cadwell and matched the lap times he had attained with his 350cc GP Yamaha. Dave Minton, testing the contraption for MCS in 1977, had it shod with plates, lights and horn for road use and inadvertently found himself cruising at 6,000rpm in complete comfort. On return, he was informed that he must have been at about 140mph!

And just how did the famed suspension work? According to Dave Minton: 'There was no change in machine attitude whatsoever during acceleration, thanks to the parallel rear suspension forks which hoiked the back end up as it tried to compress under applied power. The front remained unaffected during hard braking. No, not like an Earles fork BMW or Douglas but in a manner which left steering more or less unaffected. Nor was there any suspension movement deterioration during hard cornering. The upshot of all this is that, unlike an orthodox motorcycle, the Mead & Tomkinson racer manifests no performance decay during times of stress.'

Having cut their teeth on the Laverda triple, the Mead & Tomkinson team embarked on what came to be regarded as their masterpiece, the Kawasaki-engined special with hub-centre steering, unorthodox rear end and an underslung fuel tank into the bargain: Nessie.

For completeness it should also be recorded that a number of sidecar exponents have seen fit to rely on Laverda horses to pull their chariots, both on the road and the track. One of these specials did actually attain semi-official status in that it was factory-sponsored in the Italian and European hill-climb championships in the mid-1970s. This was a one-off built by Guilio Franzan with the assistance of another Laverda employee, Giuliano Oro. With the chair on the right-hand side in approved Continental fashion, and a fairly standard kneeler frame, Franzan's device enjoyed a considerable boon: an SFC motor!

Montjuic versus 600 SFC: Tim Parker

Unlike Raymond Ainscoe I have never owned a Montjuic; I rode one once, though, kindly loaned by Gareth Jones at Cropredy and that before I had ridden a 750 SFC. Harsh in every way, I remember. The chassis was too stiff and the powerful engine just too ragged unless smoothed out at high revs, and of course that's impractical on the street. Recalling all that now twelve or so years later has reminded me of my then final thought – what if that power were harnessed in a compliant chassis? Enter the 600 SFC.

Uwe Witt, still the Laverda importer for Germany, had sold a special sports version of the Alpino quite successfully. When factory production stopped he obviously missed the sales; after the 600 Atlas trail bike replaced it he thought he could resurrect his sports bike by taking 600 Atlas engines and put them into a suitable chassis. He chose the Harris brothers in Hertford to design and build it for him. With some difficulty they wrapped a nice mono-shock chrome-moly tube frame around the engine. Their F2 Ducati tank and seat completed their commission; Witt would add the 750 SFC replica fairing, Marzocchi forks, Brembo brakes and their own wire spoke wheels, or whatever you wanted I suppose. The idea of the 600

SFC failed when no engines became available, although five frames were made. Three became street bikes, two road racers of which one was (is) truly the 'business'. Here was that smooth, compliant Montjuic I had thought about at the Cropredy shop. The chassis is virtually faultless with White Power rear shock and any front fork, wheel, tyre combination I have tried. My engine is a numberless, oil cooler plumbed 500 crank-case bored to 583cc by Augusto Brettoni and revs freely to 11,000 (although it's not to be recommended). On the dyno I use we have seen 81 horsepower. With a Kroeber ignition it is easy to start and will even idle, more or less. On the track both engine and chassis are delightfully smooth. If only . . . of course all this is twelve years too late!

Harris-Laverda 583. Moto Witt of Cologne in Germany commissioned the Harris brothers to make Formula 2-style frame for Laverda's 500 twin. Uwe Witt's hope was that he could sell a street-legal 500 SFC with engines supplied straight from Breganze. No engines came. Five frames (this is number 5), two street bikes, two road racers, one spare frame. This is the only active road racer. It came to the USA in 1988 to be rebuilt by Steve Ferree. (Brian Nelson)

Endurance racing

With the demise of the long-distance street racing epics in 1957, Francesco Laverda called a temporary halt to his company's official involvement in road racing and more than a decade was to pass before the Breganze factory once again turned its attention to the tracks.

The impetus for the team's renaissance came, appropriately enough, from the Moto Giro d'Italia that was revived in 1967. Plainly, the event could no longer follow the lethal open roads formula of its predecessors and so it was re-cast in a seven-day rally format, with intermittent track sessions. Something in excess of 200 miles were covered each day, starting in Rome, heading south to Taranto, up along the Adriatic coast and finally back to the Eternal City. The 1967 Giro, the sixth of the post-war era, was won by one of the legendary names of Italian motorcycling, Nello Pagani. Aboard a 750cc Norton he just pipped a newcomer on the same type of machine, Augusto Brettoni, a man whose name was to become inextricably linked with Laverda's racing fortunes over the next few years.

The seventh Giro, held in April 1968, attracted 159 entrants, including a host of well-known private teams such as Scuderia Macar; but sadly the factories showed little interest in the competition beyond offering limited assistance to a number of favoured riders.

The exception to this rule was Laverda with no fewer than four of the new 650cc twins entered in Group D for bikes of over 250cc. The fledgling team reaped its just reward with Edoardo Dossena, in 8th spot overall, winning his class and his colleagues finishing respectably. With the scent of competition in their collective nostrils the Breganze teamsters were now gearing themselves up for a tilt at the endurance racing scene.

Peculiarly, although Italian companies have been, and indeed remain, at the forefront of classic road racing in its Grand Prix guise since the Continental Circus emerged in the 1920s, they – and indeed Italian race organisers – have by and large shunned endurance racing. It has long been the special preserve of the French, Belgian and Dutch circuits and enthusiasts.

However, Massimo Laverda, an arch devotee of all forms of motorcyle sport, had determined upon participation in endurance racing on the basis of the old adage that 'Racing improves the breed'. He explained his philosophy to *Motociclismo*: 'The advertising value of races, be they great or small, is immense and at the technical level the experience of racing can certainly lead to an improvement in production bikes. I maintain however that the most immediate and practical effect can be derived from endurance racing and our sporting efforts are always in that field.'

The team's race debut took place in June 1969 in the 24-hour race around a 2-mile street circuit in the industrial town of Oss in the south of Holland. The race was organised by Nederlandse Motorsport Bond, a Catholic organisation at odds with the KMNV, the Protestant body recognised by the FIM. Accordingly, the event was outlawed by the FIM and many of the riders ran under pseodonyms to protect their FIM licences. The race was notionally for international sports machines but a considerable degree of latitude was permitted.

The Laverda S of Hans Hutten was well to the fore, holding a steady third place, when forced to retire; a second 750 S then came into prominence. Massimo Laverda explains: 'We had been asked to participate by the Dutch importer and we took along three race machines and one for testing. We were faster in practice than the opposition – local Hondas, Ducatis and Guzzis – and so I decided to enter, riding the spare. It was easy to enter such a race in those days; you simply showed the organisers your driving licence and that was it. I remember that it was very foggy during the night and we found the fog a real problem, whereas the Dutch riders were used to it and of course knew the circuit.'

Massimo and his partner Brettoni had entered the event under the assumed names of 'Islero' and 'Otis' respectively. Whereas Massimo's name had just a touch of glamour, having been derived from his current sports car, Brettoni's was rather more mundane, reflecting his work as a service engineer for a lift company.

Despite a lengthy stop with a holed piston that put them way off the pace, they were determined to soldier on. After an animated debate with the organisers, they were let back into the race and claimed 4th overall behind the winning Honda, and a class victory.

Massimo should have been indulging in a champagne extravaganza in the evening but he was shattered and explained: 'It was my first, and last, 24-hour race. Although the riders could alternate every 90 minutes, it was an extremely taxing experience. My wrists were horribly swollen, thanks to the awful clutch. Indeed, I woke up during the night without any feeling whatsoever in my arms and was convinced that I was in

ABOVE **1968 and a Laverda 750 in the** *Motogiro d'Italia* **.** (Hans Blomqvist collection)

LEFT **1970 at Montlhery in France. Edoardo Dossena on a slightly modified SF during a long distance race.** (Hans Blomqvist collection)

hospital and that both arms had been amputated.'

The race confirmed Massimo's conviction that endurance racing was more than a sport: 'Deep into the race, the chain on Rizzitelli's S snapped. We had never had any difficulty before, either with the chain or indeed with our pistons, but the race found us out.'

It was in 1970 that fate smiled upon Laverda when production racing suddenly and unexpectedly came to the fore in Italy where organisers and spectators had hitherto been, at best, lukewarm towards this branch of the sport. Erstwhile racer turned journalist Vanni Blegi explained what had happened in his column in *Moto Capital*: 'In the late 1960s, most riders in Italy were still on fairly modest machines, such as Gilera 175s, and a superbike was as rare then as a speed boat is today. But a bunch of us had our bikes – a Norton Atlas, Triumph Bonneville, BSA Lightning and so on – and we passed Sundays in epic battles on the roads, racing to Genoa, with our ears to the ground. But we wanted more than that; racing called us. And so, in 1970, we put pressure on the Moto Club of Milan to put on a race for road bikes, that the spectators could associate with. In turn, the Club pressurised the FMI and obtained a permit. However, a week before the race the Club simply could not find the funds to go through with it and so all the riders underwrote the event to enable the Club to promote it without risking bankruptcy.'

The race was the 500 kilometres of Monza that

ABOVE **A modified 750 with a mixture of SFC and SF parts. The tank looks like it's made of steel, the seat fibreglass. Sergio Angiolini, victorious in the Modena 500km , 1971.**

RIGHT **Gianni Perrone aboard the factory S (or SFC?), Modena, 1971.**

proved to be a significant landmark for endurance racing in the peninsula. 10,000 spectators watched the 40 bikes, with two riders to a machine, that included Honda 4s, a singleton Guzzi V7, Triumph triples and no fewer than 10 Laverdas headed by the Augusto Brettoni-Sergio Angiolini works model that featured new brakes. When Luciano Rossi dropped the vee-twin challenger from Mandello del Lario, breaking a leg in the process, the works Laverda cleared off to take the Motociclismo Trophy with privateer S models in second and third spots.

The official factory entry was not the fastest bike in a straight line and indeed the riders reported that its handling was less that perfect, for at the Parabolica the frame seemed to flex and the bike wobbled violently. Nevertheless, the engine had one attribute eminently suited to endurance racing; it never lost its power.

The team once again entered the 24 Hours of Oss and this time came home with the bacon. Brettoni and partner Dossena led from start to finish aboard what the press described as an SF but what was in reality more of a one-off competition bike that would be developed as occasion demanded. Hans Hutten and Piet van der Wal collected the runner-up position for the Laverda importer ahead of a crowd of Dutchmen predominantly astride BMW and Honda machines.

The Italian enthusiasm for production racing really took off in 1971 and as a prelude to the Shell Gold Cup race at Imola over Easter a quality race for machines of 500cc to 1,000cc was held. The Laverda entrants faced stiff opposition on paper: the Benelli concern had sent along a brace of their new 650cc twins for Charles Mortimer and Phil Read, although Read was to be a non-starter.

Despite a fractured exhaust pipe, Brettoni rode to another of his now customary victories, just pipping Roberto Gallina aboard a private Laverda, with Mortimer languishing in their wake. The Pesaro machine was adjudged to have the superior acceleration but it lost out to the Breganze twin on top speed.

The domestic season was henceforth dominated by the newly-instituted Gino Magnani Trophy, held over a series of 500km races. With Brettoni injured, the team missed the opening round at Monza but swept back with a victory for Angiolini and Pascucci at Modena.

The victory was spoilt a little because the works Guzzi V7 of Raimondo Riva had been removed from the fray as early as the second lap, when a private Laverda cannoned into it.

Brettoni, organising the squad whilst injured, had invited his friend Gianni Perrone to ride one of the works-prepared twins at Modena. He described the machine thus: 'The bike was not really fast; it was a carthorse but the engine was unbreakable. You could do anything to it. A few years later I bought an SFC and would ride it on training sessions from my shop in Rome up to Mugello, ride round for a couple of hours and then back again. For an entire afternoon, two or three days a week for an entire winter, I used to flog that engine but it never complained. That was why they were so successful in endurance racing'.

In the third round of the series at Vallelunga, organised by the splendidly named Gentlemen's Club of Rome, the official pairing of Loigo and Bertorello took the laurels, this time actually outpacing the V7 of Brambilla and Cavalli. The press was by now describing the bikes as though they were SFCs; but the machines were almost mobile test beds and to define them too rigidly would be misleading. For instance, second-string Pascucci was riding a semi-works SFC boasting experimental 36mm Dell'Orto carburettors intended for the 1972 range.

The domestic racing scene was in truth small fry; in

Famous brochure shot of the 1972 Bol d'Or 24-hour race at Le Mans. Augusto Brettoni stands behind an SFC with racing Ceriani front brake, next to him is Roberto Gallina next to a prototype 1000 triple with Fontana front brake.

ABOVE LEFT **Barcelona 1971 for the Montjuich Park 24-hour race. SFCs came first and third. Note how this race bike still carries a horn and centre stand. This is the third place machine of Bruno Cretti and Ron Wittich.**

LEFT **A glorious shot of an unknown rider in an unknown event. Definitely a modified SF; note the missing dynamo belt.**

ABOVE **A brochure shot of the early Fontana-braked 1000 from 1972.**

1971 the squad embarked on the international circuit. Success came instantly at the 17th edition of the classic Montjuic 24 Hours around the parkland track in Barcelona. Brettoni and Angiolini moved into the lead in the tenth hour and held it to the chequered flag, ahead of the Mead & Tomkinson BSA Gold Star of Clive Brown and Nigel Rollason.

Perhaps even more telling than the outright win was the fact that two more Laverda twins survived to fill third and fourth berths. In celebratory mood, *Motociclismo* concluded its race report with the extravagant and patriotic observation: 'A handsome success this, and a victory that confirms the superiority of our country in this sector as well' (as in the GP arena, thanks to MV Agusta).

Suitably encouraged, the team passed onto the Bol d'Or, held at Le Mans, albeit over the Mickey Mouse Bugatti track instead of the celebrated Sarthe circuit. In teeming rain, Ray Pickrell and Percy Tait took a famous victory for BSA but Brettoni and Cretti rode the works Laverda to a commendable second place.

The 1972 season began with a wretched blow when Brettoni missed a gear change, fell off and wrecked his bike in a Magnani Trophy round at Modena, although at least Gallina and Pascucci salvaged some pride by taking the chequered flag.

The marque's major effort for the year was intended to be directed at the FIM's Coupe d'Endurance, the first round of which was at Barcelona. The Laverda squad was humiliated by a 360cc Bultaco ridden by Enrique Bordons and Benjamin Grau and directed by Juan Soler Bulto (who had ridden a 125cc Montesa to victory in the inaugural event in 1955). Although Brettoni had taken his habitual lead, his co-rider Pascucci dropped the SFC when the tiny Bultaco piled on the pressure.

The Breganze pairings of Gallina/Schreyer in second, Wittich/Strijbis in fourth and Bertorello/Loigo in sixth were vanquished by a motor that Bulto admitted produced a mere 36bhp and was actually in its third 24-hour race without a major overhaul. In fairness, the Bultaco probably enjoyed a weight advantage of 200 lb, which must have been the telling factor on the twisty Montjuich Park track.

No doubt duly dispirited, the factory Laverdas gave the second round, the 24 Hours of Liege at Zolder, a miss; but Raijmakers, a Dutch importer of Italian bikes, entered Ron Wittich and Doug Cash. They performed admirably to take third spot, sandwiched in the midst of four semi-works Hondas. The official FIM status of the endurance series had started to attract the major Japanese factories.

From Zolder, the circus moved on to the Zandvoort Six-Hours and tragedy. Wittch, when riding in second place, crashed after four hours and was killed. The Luton man had attained distinction racing a Norton in production events and his results earlier in the season

ABOVE **Augusto Brettoni, from just south of Florence, was a long-term Laverda road racer and contracted development engineer. He was a 'thinking' endurance racer of no mean skill and stamina, being equally fast at night as in daylight, at the end of the race as at the beginning. Here with an SFC in 1974 or 1975. (Augusto Brettoni collection)**

ABOVE RIGHT **Privateers went Laverda racing. Spa 24 hours race in 1975, two Italians, Montanari and Zocchi. The bike looks stock except for the headlamps. (Jan Heese)**

for the Raijmakers squad had been uniformly impressive.

The Bol d'Or, the jewel in the crown of endurance racing, was the team's declared target and hence, for the first time, the two fastest riders, Brettoni and Gallina, were paired together. Alas, it was to no avail and, beset by numerous trivial problems with the ignition and rear brake, they were never higher than fifth. When a piston gave up the ghost at half-distance they retired, following the Loigo/Bertorello partnership that had already exited after the latter crashed fairly heavily, fortunately without serious injury. Interestingly, a third Laverda was entered. Ridden by Tony Melody and Cash, it was a brand new 1,000cc triple; the gearbox inconsiderately failed in the fifth hour.

1973 was a distinctly lacklustre year for the team. The domestic season began with the Mille Miglia of Imola, held in two 500-mile legs under Formula 750 regulations. The Laverda machines were both outpaced and, disturbingly, unreliable, with victory going

to Continental Circus veteran Jack Findlay aboard a Suzuki managed by Suzuki Italia's overlord Roberto Patrignani. Against a Japanese mammoth, a tiny company such as Laverda had rather less chance than the proverbial snowball in Hades.

From bad to worse, for a couple of bikes were then taken along to the Magnani Trophy round at Misano. After they had set first and third fastest times in practice, the organisers pointed out that the frames had been modified at the rear. Although these modifications had fallen within the Formula 750 regulations at Imola, they offended the stricter production racing rules. The Laverda mechanics duly fitted the engines in standard frames, enabling Cazzaniga/Daneu to take second place, while colleauge Pascucci wrecked his bike in a first lap pile-up.

Internationally, the season began well at Zandvoort. The Breganze factory had not intended to participate but at the last minute was browbeaten by the Dutch importer Rinus de Groot into sending along a new SFC

complete with disc brakes for Jan Strijbis and Piet van der Wal. After a few practice laps they pronounced the machine next to useless and so ditched it in favour of their own 'SFC' that had been raced in the Oss event in 1971. They changed the forks and plundered the disc brakes from the factory model. The bike, untouched for a couple of years, ran like clockwork to win the race.

The factory's official participation, having been extremely limited thus far, now tailed off altogether, a state of affairs that continued into 1974; no doubt largely because of an early season injury sustained by Augusto Brettoni in a fall during a mountain championship race.

1974 was however notable for the emergence, on his own SFC, of a talented 21-year-old: Franco Uncini. Born in 1953, Uncini came to prominence aboard his Laverda in a series of three production races at Vallelunga. Having won the first, he was just pipped in the others by the works Ducati 750 SS and was hence launched on a career that would culminate in the 500cc world championship in 1982, aboard Roberto Gallina's Suzuki RG.

The SFC was by now outdated as a serious racing tool and the factory's future ventures would rely on the triples. Accordingly, over the winter of 1974/75 a prototype racer was tested by Ferdinando Cappellotto around the relatively tiny factory track. Although based

ABOVE **1975 Bol d'Or at Le Mans. Rider Fougeray aboard the spaceframe 1000 endurance machine fitted with the experimental 120-degree engine. He and co-rider Lucchinelli retired after 20 hours. (Hans Blomqvist collection)**

RIGHT **Now rescued by Canadian Laverda enthusiast Larry Strung for careful restoration, this is one of the 1975 180 spaceframe endurance racers 'on the street' in England in the early 1980s. (Tim Parker)**

on the production triple, numerous modifications were effected. An interesting spaceframe weighed a mere 30 lb, as against the 46 lb of the standard frame. The tubes of this frame wrapped themselves around the cylinder head and carburettors and there were no lower tubes.

The engine was revised extensively. The inlet and exhaust valves were enlarged to 40mm and 35.5mm respectively from the production 38mm and 35mm, and 36mm instead of 32mm carburettors were employed. The compression ratio was 10.9:1 instead of 9.5:1 and the innards were lightened wherever possible. Power was increased from 80bhp at 7,250rpm to 100bhp at 8,000rpm.

The alternator was switched from the right of the

crankcase to the front in the interests of handling. The racer was three inches lower than the production bike and, despite a very full race fairing that embraced the handlebars, weight had been reduced to approximately 440 lb. The orange fairing featured a horizontal dark blue stripe and two bulbous headlamps protruded.

Although not a winner, the triple performed creditably in the international arena. At the Barcelona endurance classic, the Lucchinelli/Fougeray pairing ran in second place until misfortune struck the inappropriately named Lucky, another of the emerging Italian stars to cut his teeth on Laverda racers. Touring in with a slow puncture, he was rammed by another rider. The handlebars and footrests were broken, but Fougeray was able to resume after a lengthy delay. Meanwhile, Marco Lucchinelli had been taken to hospital for a check-up, after which he was able to return to the track to help his partner to a more than creditable sixth place.

Lucchinelli and Fougeray followed up this effort with third place in the Liege 24 Hours held at Spa, while in second spot was the other team bike ridden by Roberto Gallina and Nico Cereghini (who rode for the squad on an occasional basis and was on the verge of a career with *Motociclismo*). In the season's prime event, the Bol d'Or, Lucchinelli/Fougeray and Brettoni/Cereghini were simply never in the running.

With that, Laverda pulled out of endurance racing with the triple. In 1976, Roberto Gallina took the impetuous Lucchinelli in hand, providing him with a

Suzuki RG500; and of course he too captured racing's premier championship in 1981, in Gallina colours. As for the factory, their efforts were henceforth to be concentrated on the vee-six.

1976 was to be a difficult year at Breganze, for the company's inspiration, Francesco Laverda, died in September in hospital in Thiene as a result of complications following routine surgery.

The official racing life of the triple was, however, not quite over. In 1982, a special 1,000cc RGS was developed for Italian Formula One racing. Externally, the machine differed little from the production RGS but Augusto Brettoni had supervised a multitude of internal refinements. Valve sizes were increased, revised cams were introduced and power was up to 105bhp. Three 36mm Dell'Orto carburettors were fitted instead of the 32mm standard units and a three-into-one racing exhaust system was added. Weight was a reasonable 400 lb. The machine was however stillborn internationally: the FIM shortly thereafter reduced the capacity limit for the TT and endurance championships to 750cc.

Looking back at his factory's racing team, Massimo Laverda regarded Gallina and Brettoni as his two stars: 'Gallina was a very fast GP racer, having ridden the 500cc Paton with some distinction. When he was with us, he had a Laverda dealership in La Spezia. He had an excellent technical knowledge of both frames and engines and was a determined rider. He was though

perhaps too forceful to be an absolutely top class endurance rider.'

By contrast, Augusto Brettoni never made the breakthrough into the GP arena but he was the prince among endurance racers. Massimo Laverda told how he signed on Brettoni: 'Luciano Zen and I were following the 1968 Giro in an Alfa sports car, carrying spare tyres and so on for our bikes. Mr Zen noticed Brettoni and by the end of the season we had signed him up to test our machines and to sell our bikes from his shop in Florence. He would ride between Florence and Siena on the autostrada and was constantly altering pistons and suspensions. As an endurance racer he was a maestro, following my philosophy that it is necessary to

bring a bike to the finish, because nobody remembers a retirement. Brettoni had supreme mechanical sympathy and I cannot remember him breaking an engine. His fuel consumption was always much better than our other riders. Given a full tank he would last out on the test track for at least ten minutes longer than his teammates, even though he would be just as fast.'

Although not fully-fledged factory efforts, a number of other racing episodes should be recorded. The Segoni brothers Giuliano and Roberto, from Florence, built a number of production/endurance racing specials in the 1970s, culminating in 900cc Kawasaki-engined specials that performed handsomely in the Bol d'Or. Their first creation was however based on a Laverda

SFC engine. In 1972 they came up with a spine type frame, tested by Augusto Brettoni, and in the following year they designed an aluminium monocoque frame for the Breganze twin.

In the UK, Laverdas performed honourably throughout the late 1970s, hitting the headlines in 1976 when Peter Davies rode a Jota to the Avon production racing title. Entered by Slater Brothers, the Jota raced in surprisingly standard trim. The racing tyres, revised camshaft and slightly higher compression ratio were the only concessions to the track, although the fork yokes were changed to improve high speed stability.

Mick Grant tested the Davies speedster for *Motor Cycle News* and criticised the extremely heavy throttle

ABOVE **The 500 twin was used successfully in endurance racing, at least at Montjuich Park in both 1978 and 1979, winning the 500 class. This is Brettoni (co-rider Pete Davies) aboard in 1978.** (*Motociclismo)*

LEFT **Formula 1 racing in Italy in 1984 was joined by one factory RGS. Here's one of (probably) two bikes developed in the factory prototype shop.** (Tim Parker)

and the difficulty in engaging first gear. Those features apart, he was impressed: 'I must admit, I had expected a wrestling match. Apart from a little wobble, handling was absolutely superb.'

The Jota went on to further successes in UK production racing, with Davies, Mick Hunt and Roger Winterburn well to the fore in the Avon championships; and in 1978 Lennart Backstrom annexed the Swedish production title.

Meanwhile, revised Alpino machines had earned some repute on the endurance stage. Looking like miniature SFCs, having poached their tank and seat, and sporting a half fairing mounted to the frame, two factory-entered 500s were ridden by Brettoni/Davies and Barba/Ricart to 9th and 10th overall in the Barcelona 24 Hours of 1978. The first pair's class victory at the Montjuich circuit (or 'Montjuic' in Catalan), prompted the choice of name for the raucous Slater Brothers-inspired road bike.

The factory Alpino-based 500cc bikes were ridden to further successes in 1979, with Augusto Brettoni and his brother Filippo taking second and third places in the Italian production championship. Amazingly, the Brettoni/Davies and Barba/Ricart pairings exactly reproduced their previous year's placings in the Barcelona marathon.

Laverdas have also competed with some distinction in the TT since their first appearance in 1972 when Jeff Wade took a silver replica in the Formula 750 race. Other highlights down the years included Mick Hunt's

sixth place aboard his Jota in the 1977 Formula One race and the similar place attained by Peter Davies in the 1978 Formula Two event on the 500cc racer.

The 1980 F2 race was almost a Laverda benefit with seven Formula 500/Montjuic steeds in the first fourteen, with Davies 5th, George Fogarty 7th, Lennart Backstrom 9th, Hunt 11th, Bernard Murray 12th, Winterburn 13th and journalist Ray Knight 14th. As late as 1982 and 1983 Malcolm Wheeler was able to ride his early-Harris-framed Montjuic, taken out to near 600cc, to 4th and 5th places respectively in the F2 four-lapper.

In the mid- and late-1980s Laverdas have been well to the fore in Battle of the Twins and Classic events. When in 1983 the BOTT series was launched, two Laverdas were particularly prominent: Steve Elliott's 750cc SFC with a Motodd engine and Maurice Ogier's Montjuic bored out to 592cc. The latter machine, ridden by journalist Alan Cathcart and others, was notable for a special fuel tank placed under the seat, and a dummy shroud sitting over the engine at one point. In final form it had a Hossack frame.

As the 1990s began, Laverdas still roamed the tracks, predominantly in Classic events. With the large capacity production classes banned from the TT, the prospects for witnessing a Breganze product once again in the greatest of open roads races must be remote; but, for lovers of the Mountain course, a singleton modified SFC, ridden by Tom Quaye, graced the Manx GP in 1990.

LEFT Mountain climbing is a popular competition in Italy. Stefano Pagnozzi 'dirt-tracking' a Brettoni-prepared 500 twin in the 500 class, often beating many a GP Suzuki on the way.

ABOVE Like the 750 and 1000s, the 500 made an interesting road racer. Perhaps the fastest machine built was Maurice Ogier's which did well all over Europe as an F2 bike, in the Isle of Man, and at Daytona where it won the 1984 Battle of the Twins with Alan Cathcart riding. Here it's using the stock frame, also with Alan riding, somewhere in Europe. (Kel Edge)

The vee-six

Occasionally, a blue-blooded thoroughbred racing motorcycle emerges that subsequently enters into the consciousness of enthusiasts as being technically way ahead of its time and which, it has to be said, more often than not turns out to be a glorious failure. The most outstanding example of such a beast may well be Moto Guzzi's 500cc vee-eight of the mid-1950s and the genre has undoubtedly been kept alive more recently by the innovative Elf series. A serious contender for a place in the lists amongst such worthies must be Laverda's vee-six 1,000cc endurance racer. Like the legendary Guzzi, the Laverda never attained anywhere near its full potential and indeed this near mythical motorcylce raced only once: in the 1978 Bol d'Or.

The vee-six originated in the mid-1970s when Massimo realised that the possibilities of the existing twin and three cylinder ranges had been exhausted. He and Luciano Zen decided to experiment with a multi-cylinder engine featuring water-cooling, shaft drive, electronic ignition and four valve heads, with the underlying intention that the products of their research should be channelled into a new generation of road bikes.

It would be satisfying to be able to record that the vee-six was quite simply the logical product of these requirements, but the truth was rather more complex. The key to the choice of a vee-six motor was to be found in the background of one of the designers, Giulio Alfieri.

Having graduated from the Milan Polytechnic College in the late 1940s, Alfieri soon found himself working for the mammoth Innocenti combine on a host of aircraft and industrial engines. Here he met chief engineer Pier Luigi Torre who poached him for the experimental department to breathe on Lambretta engines. At that time Lambretta, an important branch of the Innocenti empire, was in the middle of a highly publicised record-breaking contest against the rival Vespa concern. Lambretta engaged top notch riders such as Romolo Ferri, Dario Ambrosini and Umberto Masetti who duly appropriated a host of 125cc speed records on what was in effect little more than a souped-up scooter.

It was while testing these machines at the Modena autodrome that Alfieri met Camillo Donati, who was Maserati's lawyer. Within a short time he had moved to the quality car manufacturer. His contacts with the motorcycle fraternity were not altogether broken, for in Italy there was a considerable amount of cross-fertilisation between the two-wheel and four-wheel industries. For instance, at Maserati he worked with Gioacchino Colombo, a consultant engineer engaged to design the celebrated world championship winning 250F and who subsequently went on to work for MV Agusta. Alfieri's career progressed apace and by the age of 30 he was Maserati's technical director.

For a number of years Maserati trod a financial tightrope. One source of salvation was a link with the French Citroen concern. In 1972 Maserati unveiled the Merak, a coupe produced in reaction to Citroen's understandable desire that a Maserati car should be something more than a thing of beauty and should actually sell in sufficient numbers to generate a profit.

It was decreed that the Merak's engine should be a vee-six but the power plant that emerged featured several oddities, not the least of which was the 90-degree angle between the banks. Citroen was desperate for results and so, instead of allowing Alfieri to design a vee-six from scratch, one cylinder was simply lopped off each bank of an existing experimental 2,965cc vee-eight that he had laid down in 1965. The resultant vee-six, with its 90-degree angle, produced uneven firing intervals, as a 60-degree or 120-degree angle is required for even firing intervals in a vee-six in which each pair of connecting rods share a crankpin.

Alfieri gained a considerable wealth of experience working on Maserati's engines and was regarded as one of the leading authorities on the combustion process with an unrivalled knowledge concerning fuel atomisation, cylinder filling, valve angles, port layout, valve timing and so on.

By the early 1970s, the Maserati company was losing

There's no question that multi-cylinder engines can capture the imagination of all enthusiasts. With today's blandness in four, only six or more would do. Moto Laverda stole the show in the 1970s with its vee-six. The engine, seen here on the factory dynomometer, was powerful and in itself successful even if the whole motorcycle wasn't. The exhaust note is music.

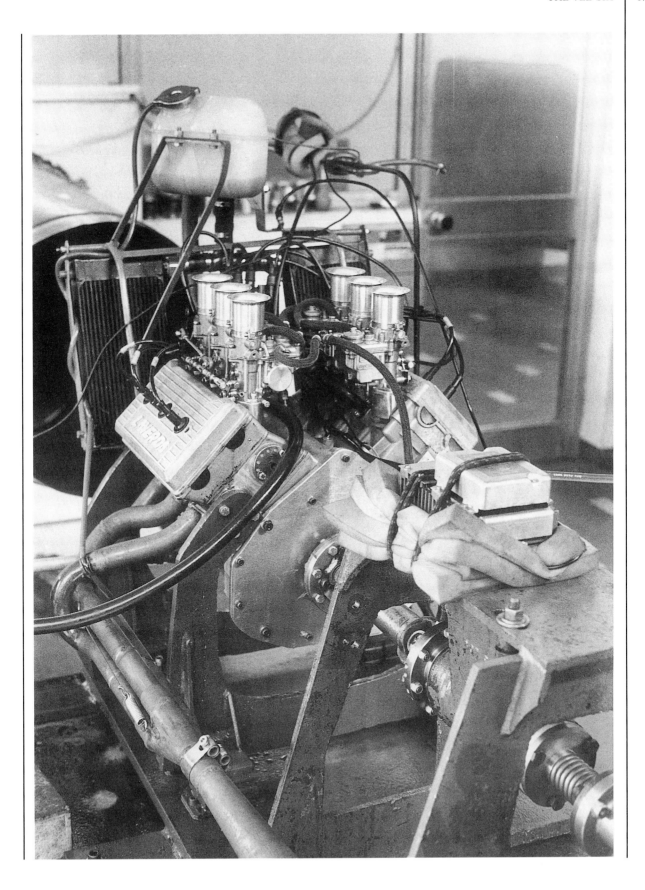

OPPOSITE ABOVE **Factory press shot of the show 'cantilever' vee-six. Note the beautiful downdraught Weber carburettors, the massive ignition pack and all the familiar parts from a multitude of Laverda production models. The show bike is believed not to exist in this form anymore.**

OPPOSITE BELOW **No wonder the world stood back in shock when this prototype was first revealed. The show bike was purposeful, if not raceable; strange combination of treaded front tyre and rear slick.**

LEFT **From the rear the show bike isn't slim. In the flesh, however, it isn't all that bulky either. The bevel drive rear hub is quite obvious here.**

LEFT Still the same show bike, on show in Milan in 1978, with the lower half of the fairing removed. Here the cantilever rear suspension is on view; the rear spring is under the engine. We all wanted to know if it would go into production.

RIGHT The only other completed vee-six was the Bol d'Or endurance racer seen here at the start of the race in 1978. Perugini and Cereghini struggled for 10 of the 24 hours until the bike broke. Note the changes from the show bike; headlamps, fairing and most markedly the rear suspension; now twin rear shocks used conventionally on a massively braced swingarm. (Jim Greening)

lire hand over fist and was in and out of the bankruptcy courts. Citroen, angling for an opt-out, found a welcome saviour in the form of the Argentinian entrepreneur Alejandro de Tomaso, sometime overlord of the remnants of the Guzzi and Benelli empires. In August 1975, within days of de Tomaso's takeover, a shocked Alfieri was dismissed.

He then plumped for a spell as a freelance consultant and was thus lured to Laverda by Massimo whom he had known since the latter's days in Modena, when Massimo had inveigled his way into the Maserati design shop. Alfieri was engaged to work at Breganze for one day a week with the brief of imparting new ideas and his input was critical as regards the concept of what was outwardly a new endurance racer, but what was in reality a mobile test bed.

The machine was conceived by Massimo, Zen and Alfieri during 1976 and was revealed to expectant journalists in the following year; an example was unveiled to the public at the Milan Show at the tail end of 1977.

The engine and transmission unit were made in the Laverda family's foundry at Gallarate. The six cylinders were arranged in two banks of three with a 90-degree angle inherited from its Maserati forebear. The oversquare dimensions of 65×50mm gave a capacity of 165.98cc per cylinder, 995.89cc in total.

There were four valves per cylinder set at 28 degrees with 24mm diameter for the inlets and 23.5mm for the exhausts. There was a single 10mm plug for each cylinder.

Initially, a Lucas fuel injection system was favoured but this was soon replaced by six Dell'Orto carburettors installed between the banks.

Originally 30mm units were selected but 32mm versions were fitted after tests. The twin overhead camshafts were governed by two chains – again, a Maserati characteristic – running off a shaft that in turn was chain-driven off the front of the longitudinally placed single piece crankshaft.

There were two separate oil pumps driven off the front of the crank with one pressure pump and the other to scavenge the five-litre dry sump system. The oil tank was housed beneath the seat and there was a single large oil cooler in front of the cylinder block. There were two large water radiators to service the six-litre cooling system.

A Marelli distributor sat behind the steering head and worked with an electronic ignition unit that had been designed originally for use on a Ferrari vee-twelve GP car to provide a high intensity spark for running at revs in excess of 10,000 rpm.

The electric starter, electric fuel pump and endurance lighting system – that powered two headlamps of a type used as a spotlight option for the Porsche 911 – required a generator to charge the substantial 12-volt battery which was mounted beside the oil tank on the right-hand side, under the seat. The five-speed gearbox featured a left foot change.

Compared to the ambitious and innovative power plant, the cycle parts were distinctly old hat and certainly the thinking behind them was nowhere near as radical as that displayed on the virtually contemporary French Elf X endurance racer. The engine was employed as a stressed member and was bolted to a tubular frame (the most subtantial part of which was the spine), and which carried the front suspension. There was a rear sub-frame carrying the seat.

Originally a swinging fork enclosed the drive shaft in the right arm with the suspension provided by means of

a single damper unit mounted horizontally along the crankshaft axis underneath the gearbox. Front suspension was courtesy of conventional Marzocchi 38mm units. Campagnolo wheels were shod with Dunlop tyres, measuring 4 × 18in and 5 × 18in in front and rear respectively. Twin Brembo discs were fitted at the front and one at the rear, all of which were 280mm versions.

On paper, all looked well and the engine, in its first test, produced an encouraging 118bhp, so that the target of 140bhp seemed to be well within reach. But once this formidable engine was mated to the cycle parts, the team's problems began.

The use of a longitudinal crankshaft inevitably entailed an adverse torque reaction as the engine rotated across the frame. The designers appreciated the difficulty, already experienced by the Guzzi riders with the Mandello stable's vee-twin, but they had underestimated its effects when allied to an engine delivering something in excess of 120bhp. The test riders found the bike simply unrideable.

Accordingly, the gearbox was placed to one side and a reduction gear was fitted to the clutch which thereby rotated in an opposite direction to the crankshaft, cancelling out some of its forces.

The torque reaction was also causing the rear wheel to rise and fall violently under rapid acceleration and deceleration, so the experimental suspension system

was discarded in favour of a conventional twin shock rear end using Marzocchi units.

The transmission crankcase casings were also redesigned to enable the new swinging arm to pivot on the perceived centre of gravity. A drawback was the necessity of introducing a two-piece drive shaft with a universal joint coupling the two halves.

The statistics obtained during the testing undertaken during 1978 were encouraging: usable power came in at 4,000rpm and maximum power was the intended 140bhp at 11,800rpm. Engine development had concentrated on yielding a wide power band, rather than maximum bhp, and Alfieri was of the opinion that 160bhp would have been attainable. Fuel economy was also noteworthy, thanks to the efficient combustion generated by the paired valves, narrow valve angle and flat top alloy pistons.

The squad's target was the 24 hour classic, the Bol d'Or, the fifth round of the FIM's Coupe d'Endurance, that was to be held at the Paul Ricard circuit in mid-September. It had been switched from the Le Mans Bugatti circuit because of political bickering within the French federation.

In the interests of reliability the engine was de-tuned and the final tests indicated 138.7bhp at 10,500 rpm. The bike's Achilles heel was its weight. In an attempt to save much-needed funds, Massimo had steered clear of

indulging in expensive magnesium castings and titanium components. With oil, water and fuel the machine tipped the scales at 520 lb, of which the engine-gearbox unit registered a massive 385 lb.

As an illuminating contrast, the Yamaha TZ750E, entered by Sonauto for Patrick Pons and Christian Sarron, weighed little over 320 lb. In fairness, Massimo conjectured that had lightweight materials been employed, the weight of the marque's new flagship racer could have been slashed by at least 100 lb.

The vee-six was however compact, with a wheelbase of 57 inches, a seat height of 29 and a maximum width of 21, making it narrower than a number of its Japanese competitors. It was clothed with a half-fairing and finished in traditional vivid orange.

For the carnival that was the Bol, the selected riders were Nico Cereghini, by now an experienced Laverda endurance racer, and Carlo Perugini, that year's Italian 500cc champion aboard a Suzuki RG and just embarking on his GP career.

The Bol was notable for the speed and reliability of the two-stroke Yamaha with which Pons and Sarron humiliated the assembled Honda RCB opposition for over half the race, until the motor cried enough, handing the race to the Honda pairing of Leon and Chemarin.

Meanwhile, the Laverda's drive shaft's universal joint failed after eight hours. Instead of replacing it and setting off again, the team called it a day, satisfied with the data obtained.

The most spectacular statistic to be gleaned was that of the projectile's speed through the mile-long Mistral straight trap: a phenomenal 176mph, faster than the works Yamaha and 19mph up on the next four-stroke, one of the works Hondas. Massimo was convinced that with increased revs and different gearing another 10mph could have been extracted, that would have taken the motorcycle beyond the magic 300km/h barrier.

After that solitary public performance, the racer was consigned to the relative oblivion of display in the factory's entrance hall. A spare engine found a resting place in Massimo's living room in his house on the outskirts of Breganze, while bits and pieces of a third motor were still lying around in the factory a dozen years later.

There was however a postscript to the tale. In 1980, Rene Siccardi, a self-made millionaire operating as a sub-contractor within the French automobile industry, decided to diversify by designing and building a three-cylinder 1,000cc dohc superbike, which saw the light of day in 1981.

At a preliminary stage, however, Siccardi turned to Italy for know-how, approaching Bimota for assistance with the frame. A clash of Latin temperaments put paid to that, and Siccardi then sought to acquire the now defunct Laverda vee-six project in its entirety.

Negotiations were so far advanced that Siccardi's designer, Francois Nadim, spent three months at the Breganze factory discussing the machine. Abruptly, Piero Laverda pulled out of the deal, for the ostensible reason that he was not happy to see the vee-six developed alongside and in competition with Siccardi's own three-cylinder engine. For what it was worth, Nadim was convinced that Luciano Zen was jealous of the exciting project (essentially Alfieri's brainchild), and talked Piero into killing it off.

The press speculated during the late 1970s that the racer would be a precursor to a vee-six road bike but Massimo vehemently denied this, pointing out that it

LEFT **Augusto Brettoni, centre, with the vee-six at the Bol d'Or.**

BELOW **Once in a while the vee-six is exercised for the admiring around the factory test track. Severely overgeared, still wearing its 1978 Bol d'Or slicks and without the benefit of tuning it still 'makes the earth move' as it rips around, here in 1984. (Tim Parker)**

would have been prohibitively expensive for the financially-stricken factory to set up the required new tooling. Instead, by deciding at the outset not to go into production, Massimo allowed his team complete freedom of design, as Zen and Alfieri were unfettered by the constraints that would have been imposed by the concerns of translating their ideas into a production run.

For all Massimo's denials, the story of the vee-six might not end in 1978. In 1989, Nuova Moto Laverda's commercial director Paolo Bauducco revealed that the company that had arisen from the ashes of the family enterprise, proposed to put the vee-six engine to use: 'We can go in two directions. First, to produce a limited number, perhaps 150, of replicas updated in the cycle parts but substantially unchanged mechanically. In the longer term, three production bikes could be based on it. We have in mind a 1,100cc vee-six, a 750cc vee-four and an in-line 600cc triple, all of which could be easily derived from the existing engine.'

The company's technical director Angelo Ferrari added that the project was at the preliminary stage and that there were a number of decisions still to be taken: for example, whether to persist with the shaft drive or to turn the engine through 90 degrees and opt for a chain final drive. Ferrari was however convinced that the vee-six would enable the factory to produce a range of motors relatively easily. The middle capacity triple could be one bank of the flagship 1,100cc bike's engine, while the vee-four could be produced by lopping off two of the cylinders from the vee-six. Thus, some fifteen years after its conception, the endurance racer was actually on the verge of inspring a range of road bikes.

CHAPTER

Nuova Moto Laverda

By 1984 the harassed company was undoubtedly, in a phrase beloved of Italians, *in crisi*, in crisis. Annual production of the entire 125cc range, that had been planned at the marque's saviour, was barely over three thousand, while that of the standard bearing 1,000cc triples was measured in hundreds rather than thousands. The flagging sales coincided with crippling expenditure on tooling for the new models that were to emerge over the next couple of years, not to mention the punishing costs associated with the production of a multi-purpose four-wheel-drive vehicle which would prove to be virtually unsellable.

Hand in hand with these internal difficulties, the hitherto protected Italian lightweight market was undergoing a siege as the Japanese sought a backdoor entry in order to avoid the swingeing tariff barriers imposed on the import of motorcycles under 400cc. But whereas Aprilia, Cagiva and Gilera were already embarking on imaginative programmes that would culminate in the launch of an exciting and popular range of 125cc race replicas before the end of the decade, Massimo and Piero were reputedly almost literally at each other's throats.

As a host of creditors constantly badgered for payment, news of the company's cash flow problems and financial malaise soon entered the public domain. Although it was strenuously denied at the time, the family shareholders received a number of serious bids from both Japanese and American companies, anxious to establish a toe-hold in the Italian market by assembling their products in the peninsula, thereby avoiding the tariff barriers. The negotiations floundered as the would-be purchasers weighed the costs against the potential profits.

At this stage, hopes of salvation were pinned on a new superbike range. By February 1984 all the design work had been completed and indeed a wooden mock-up was displayed, illustrating the format of a transverse four-cylinder 16-valve engine. The water-cooled cylinders were inclined forwards at about 30 degrees and the alternator was to be placed behind them to reduce width. Two power plants were envisaged: a 1,000cc unit, with cylinder sizes of 53×77.5mm and a 750cc edition with the same 53mm bore but a 67mm stroke. It was hoped that the smaller version could be tailored to participate in the endurance racing world championship. Sadly, by March 1984 the company's parlous financial state forced these proposals onto the back burner.

By the start of 1985 the wolf was at the factory gates and could be appeased no longer. Hence, an application was made to the commercial courts in Vicenza for a form of court-controlled administration. This procedure is perhaps akin to the English 'administration' and under it, for a pre-determined period, a court-appointed administrator ran the company along pre-arranged lines. Trading activities were restricted and the administrator's primary duty was to return the business to profitable status in the short term to enable the creditors to be paid off. The advantage of this mechanism was that the creditors were prevented from pressing their claims for the set period of grace.

Initially, Laverda applied for a 24-month stay of execution. This was granted by the court on the basis that the exciting 350cc and 500cc vee-three projects should have been producing the goods within that timescale. It was originally intended to axe the mighty 1,000cc triple but, as it remained the best selling Italian superbike in Britain, this misguided policy was short lived. Piero Laverda duly spent the autumn of 1985 visiting the European concessionaires, assuring them that a limited production run of the triple would see the light of day, with a total of 300 proposed for 1986 and 1987, of which 50 or 60 were to be allocated to Britain.

Under the controlled administration, Massimo's direct involvement came to an end but Piero assumed the role of president, acting as a figurehead at prestige shows and press conferences. The production figures for 1986 were 300 triples, nearly 1,000 of the OR Atlas tiddlers and almost 3,000 of the 125cc models; hardly sufficient to stave off the creditors indefinitely.

As late as autumn 1986, with time running out, the

ABOVE RIGHT **Nuova Moto Laverda in 1989 launched their new models with the slogan 'The legend is coming back, passion too'. The styling of the new models was, frankly, radical; this little 50 enduro called the Gaucho the tamest of them all. It carried a Cagiva engine, designated 50 CR-2.**

RIGHT **The 125 custom model was called the Toledo.**

directors were still pontificating to the Italian press about the latest projects to issue forth from the pen of engineer Bocchi, such as a four-stroke vee-twin engine and a water-cooled dohc 350cc single-cylinder motor. Alas, it was not to be, and in February 1987 the company was in the receivership court in Vicenza. Some months later, the court took full responsibility when it assumed ownership of Moto Laverda s.r.l., with its land, machinery, warehouses full of bikes, spare parts, drawings, technical archives and projects.

The Tribunale at Vicenza appointed a receiver whose concern was to find a purchaser and to use the proceeds of sale to settle the company's debts. The receiver inevitably ran the business without incurring any unnecessary risks, merely selling off spare parts and authorising minimal production.

The receiver negotiated with a number of interested parties, and eventually dealt with a group of existing employees who were keen to run what might be best described as a workers' cooperative. In July 1988 the

ABOVE **The 125 sport, the Navarro, had an electric starter and seven speeds if only to keep up with the likes of Cagiva. Unadvertised was the fact that Laverda had bought Cagiva engines to power it!**

ABOVE RIGHT **El Cid was the would-be successor to the Atlas, now with 700cc apparently, and fuel injection.**

would-be entrepreneurs formed a new company, Nuova Moto Laverda, as the vehicle for their intended buy-out. Unfortunately, delays in putting together the financial arrangements meant that it was not until 2 May 1989 that the new company was able to buy the remnants of its predecessor and start trading.

First and foremost, some 65 employees put in a reported £8,000 each, with another £3,000 due as a second instalment at a later date. This was sufficient to give the employee-shareholders 75% of the equity in

the new venture, and together with funds provided by a finance company and low-interest government loan it was sufficient to enable the receiver to pay off outstanding debts.

Outside investors took the remaining 25% stake, the maximum shareholding that such investors can take in a cooperative under Italian company law.

Surprisingly, and worryingly, the theme common to the new hierarchy was the complete absence of any previous motorcycle industry experience. The new president, being its titular head without having day-to-day executive responsibility, was 32-year-old Ugo Holzer. With an economics degree from Venice, he was in essence a politician, a councillor in Vicenza and vice-president of an association of such cooperatives in the surrounding Veneto region.

The commercial director was a 60-year-old mechanical engineer, Paolo Bauducco, whose previous specialisation had been in promoting exports for a local business consortium. One of his functions was to

protect, so far as possible, the investment of the oustide shareholders in Nuova Moto Laverda. In their turn, the employees were represented by a long-serving factory stalwart, Nicola Lievore, who had already worked for the company for over twenty years.

A particularly heavy burden was placed on the shoulders of the new technical director, Angelo Ferrari, whose former engineering experience had been garnered lately at Lamborghini.

The primary objective of the fledgling company was nothing more ambitious than survival, but a handsome chunk of the available capital was invested in sophisticated up-to-the-minute machinery which was used to produce a new range at the Milan Show in November 1989. In essence, however, the five models that were on offer were nothing more exciting than thinly disguised updates of existing offerings, with exotic sounding Spanish names bestowed upon them to add spice.

The Minarelli-engined 50cc enduro-styled bike was dubbed the Gaucho while the revamped 125cc machin-

ery was the five-speed Toledo custom bike, relying on the engine that had started life in the Lesmo range, and the Navarro sports version.

The Navarro was equipped with a seven-speed gearbox allied to a power-valve Cagiva motor sitting within a square-section steel frame. The bike featured a single-shock suspension and single disc brakes and was fully faired with an eye-catching bright red, white and blue colour scheme. *Bike* magazine described the sporster as 'not so much a race-replica as a juvenile delinquent's version of the Honda CBR600' but concluded that 'compared to the alloy-framed 125cc exotica currently on offer from the likes of Aprlia and Gilera, the Navarro is a shade basic and untrendy'.

Nearest to original projects were two so-called 700cc steeds. Some modest engine development had been undertaken on the virtually antique 180-degree eight-valve dohc twin-cylinder engine that had started life in the Alpino. It had been taken out to 78.5 × 69mm to produce an actual 668cc. The enduro version, dubbed 'El Cid', enjoyed six speeds and Weber-Marelli electronic fuel injection. 60bhp at 7,500rpm was available to produce a claimed 120mph. The companion model was the custom 'Hidalgo' which, relying on 36mm Keihin carburettors, delivered 10bhp less.

The 700 Hidalgo (actually 668cc) was a larger custom model similar in style to the Toledo. Japanese Keihin carburettors were used. Top speed was quoted at 99mph.

The reaction of the Italian agents to this new range was less than ecstatic. The looks of the machines were undoubtedly controversial, as Angelo Ferrari freely admitted. There seemed to be a deliberate policy of producing dramatic looking bikes in order to ensure that Laverda would hit the headlines, presumably on the basis that there is no such thing as bad publicity.

The styling was the work of a young Frenchman, Djamel Mocheri, who in keeping with his colleagues had no previous motorcycle experience. Although one or two scribes kindly opined that the styling was an acquired taste, the overwhelming critical response was damning. Perhaps typical was *Superbike*'s reaction that the El Cid was 'by far the best looking of the lot, which unfortunately does not say much'. The magazine pulled no punches, describing the general styling as 'unbelievably brutish and ugly', with the Hidalgo considered 'hideous' and the Navarro a 'bulbous little beast'.

In the short term, the company had to sell its new

machines together with the remnants of the bikes that came from the receiver, and indeed provide a comprehensive spare parts service for the beloved 750cc SF range and the triples, in order to stay afloat. The company's need for cash was so pressing that vast discounts were offered to shift stock.

The directors appreciated that the company was merely treading water and even a medium-term campaign would have been over-ambitious. If, however, the directors had a plan, it was that the company should revert to type and cash in on its reputation as a manufacturer of quality, large-capacity motorcycles. Hence, they revived the popular 1,000cc SFC as an interim measure and then proposed the new 668cc twin-cylinder engine. And perhaps most encouraging for the Laverda enthusiast was the announcement of the possibility of a range of engines based on the vee-six endurance racer.

But, away from pipe-dreams and back in the world of harsh economic reality, rumours of yet further cash-flow problems bedevilling the infant company started to filter through to the press in the early months of 1990. By the time of the Cologne Show at the tail end of the year, there were firm indications that a Japanese company had acquired a 51% shareholding and intended to employ the name as a marketing device to promote a range of fashionware.

In January 1991, part, but probably not all, off the truth came to light. Called by Laverda's brand new president, Nicola Lievore who had been promoted from within, a Breganze press conference announced a joint venture between the Zanini Group, a Vincenza-based merchant bank with a 25% stake in Nuova Moto Laverda, and Shinken Corporation, a retail wing of a giant Tokyo-based engineering company. To operate in Japan in the guise of Kabushiki Kaisha Laverda Japan, the primary function of the new company was seemingly to build and market a vee-six Nissan-engined Group C racing car, in street legal form: a far cry indeed from the principles that had inspired Francesco Laverda to produce his run-abouts!

On the motorcycling front, the collaborators' proposals included the production of a limited edition of exact replicas of Alfieri's vee-six endurance racer: 25 bikes at £37,000 apiece was the original intention, but after a couple of months emerged a suggestion that 100 machines would be available at £25,000 each the same price as Bimota's top-of-the-range Tesi, the very last word in exclusivity. Hints of a new sports bike, possibly with an updated 668cc dohc Montjuic-type parallel twin power plant and a Nico Bakker frame, were also thick on the ground. As the cliché has it, only time will tell.

But, whatever the future may hold, what a legacy will have been left to motorcycling folklore by this tiny factory in Breganze. Beautiful gem-like 75cc racers dominating long-distance epics in the 1950s; the 750cc SFC, an instant classic; the mighty, cult Jota; the raucous Montjuic, the unique vee-six; all, in their own distinctive and stylish manner, things of beauty and joys forever.

Appendix: Specifications

SPECIFICATIONS

Model	75	750 SFC	Chott	Jota	Montjuic	SFC 1,000
Year	1956	1971	1974	1977	1980	1988
Bore	46mm	80mm	68mm	75mm	72mm	75mm
Stroke	45mm	72mm	68mm	74mm	61mm	74mm
Cylinders	1	2	1	3	2	3
Capacity	74.78cc	743.92cc	246.9cc	981cc	496.7cc	981cc
bhp	7	70	26	90	n/a	84
rpm	9,600	7,500	7,600	7,600	n/a	7,000
c.r.	9.7:1	9.6:1	10:1	10:1	9:1	10:1
valves	ohv	sohc	2 stroke	dohc	dohc	dohc
Gears	3/4	5	5	5	6	5
Top speed	80mph	135mph	n/a	141mph	107mph	140mph

OVERLEAF Alan Cathcart winning the 'Battle of the Twins', Daytona, 1984. Maurice Ogier's machine, still under 600cc, blew by the 750s. (Don Morley)

PAGE 188 The inimitable 500cc Montjuic. (Don Morley)

PAGE 189 Silver-framed 1000 Jota, 1979; in the middle distance, a dealer special, the Cropredy Liberator; behind it, a 1983 1000 RGS. (Tim Parker)

Index